Remembering
Roy E. Disney

MEMORIES AND PHOTOS OF A STORIED LIFE

REMEMBERING
ROY E. DISNEY

MEMORIES AND PHOTOS OF A STORIED LIFE

By DAVID A. BOSSERT
FOREWORD BY ROY PATRICK DISNEY

Disney Editions

New York • Los Angeles

For information address Disney Editions,
1101 Flower Street, Glendale, California 91201

Designed by Winnie Ho and ARLENE SCHLEIFER GOLDBERG

ISBN 978-1-4231-7805-7
G475-5664-5-13200
Printed in the United States of America
Reinforced binding
First Edition
10 9 8 7 6 5 4 3 2 1

Visit www.disneybooks.com

D23
The Official Disney Fan Club
Disney.com/D23

SUSTAINABLE FORESTRY INITIATIVE   Certified Sourcing
www.sfiprogram.org
SFI-00993

THIS LABEL APPLIES TO TEXT STOCK

For
Nancy, Sydney, and Marlee

Table of Contents

Acknowledgments

I am sincerely grateful to many individuals for their unwavering support and selfless efforts in helping me complete this book project. Although a writer is often envisioned as a solitary individual sitting at a keyboard, writing is in fact much more participatory than that. Yes, I did write much of this book on long-haul flights and while alone in upper midcoast Maine, but I also spent many hours speaking with various individuals who knew Roy E. Disney.

This book would not have happened if it were not for the suggestion Don Hahn made that I put this collection of stories together. Don has been a longtime friend and colleague at Disney. His tutelage, advice, and counsel have been invaluable over the years, and that impact is no more evident than in the completion of this book.

Don also referred me to one of the most wonderful publishing executives, Wendy Lefkon. Her steadfast guidance and passion about this book were both greatly appreciated and thoroughly educating. Wendy's dry sense of humor and intellectual depth were both integral and essential to wading into the publishing world and process.

This book also could not have moved forward without the approval and cooperation of Roy Patrick Disney and his siblings, Tim, Susan, and Abigail. Roy Patrick was immediately supportive of this book celebrating his father, and gracious in writing the Foreword. Leslie DeMeuse Disney, Roy's widow, approved as well, and I am very appreciative for their faith and trust in me to do a loving tribute to Roy Edward Disney.

Stanley Gold, Roy's business partner at Shamrock Holdings, Inc., was very generous with his time to share some stories. He welcomed me into his home and was very insightful into many of Roy's pivotal moments and his involvement at The Walt Disney Company.

Robbie Haines, who sailed with Roy for many years, was also quite generous with many of their sailing adventures. His stories and photos from aboard Roy's beloved *Pyewacket* have added a wonderful facet to this book.

Peter Schneider and Thomas Schumacher, who together headed up the Walt Disney Animation Studios during the bulk of what is now acknowledged to be the "Second Golden Age of Disney Animation," were invaluable in their insights and clarity. Their support and sharing of stories were important and gratefully included.

John Lasseter, the chief creative officer of Pixar and Disney, was also very helpful in sharing a number of stories.

His insights and remembrances of Roy were thoroughly enjoyable to listen to, and several are sprinkled throughout this book.

I also received a lot of help and encouragement from my Disney colleagues Ed Nowak, Howard Green, and George Scribner, as well as Cameron Ramsay and Ashleigh Bateman. Justin Arthur from Disney Corporate Archives was a tremendous help in finding a number of rarely seen photos of Roy early in his career at the Disney Studios.

Finally, heartfelt thanks to my wife, Nancy, and our daughters, Sydney and Marlee, and my parents, Philip and Virginia, as well as my siblings, Phil Jr., Caroline, and Alison.

—Dave Bossert
Burbank, California 2013

A very young Roy E., center, with blond hair on the tricycle, circa 1933

Foreword

On an early fall evening in 1937, seven-year-old Roy Edward Disney was in bed fighting a cold. His Uncle Walt had come from work to visit Roy's mom and dad—my grandparents, Edna and Roy Oliver Disney. Walt sat on the edge of young Roy's bed and told a story. As my father remembered it, Walt went on for several hours telling him the story of a little wooden boy. At the time, Walt had been in the middle of doing storyboards for *Pinocchio*, one of the greatest animated movies ever made. Ah, to be a fly on the wall that evening!

Walt Disney, the man, it has been posited, was the perfect marriage of art and industry. Born at the turn of the twentieth century, when nearly half the country was still agrarian, he was a blend of Mark Twain and Henry Ford. He was a storyteller and marketer almost without equal.

Unu 16 (93 o

*Young Roy E. Disney with his
mother (far left and below), Edna*

*Roy E. Disney
with cat, circa
late 1930s*

Roy Edward Disney was born on January 10, 1930. The only child of older parents (mother Edna was forty and father Roy O. was thirty-seven), Roy was born into the middle of an explosion in the film business. His father, Roy Oliver, was Walt's older brother and business partner, and it was his job to find a way to finance movies and techniques that in many cases had never been tried before. Roy Oliver also helped invent both character marketing and foreign distribution. It turned into a unique and broad education for my father, Roy Edward Disney.

*Young Roy E. with his father, Roy O. Disney, and the family dog (above)
and with his mother, Edna (top)*

And thank goodness my dad had an insatiable hunger to learn. Home movies, for instance, were a rare commodity in the American home in 1930, but movie cameras were ubiquitous in the Disney household. World travel, especially by air, was difficult and trying at best. Roy Oliver built and expanded a business through world travel, and my father was fortunate to go along on many of these journeys. He was in Mexico City and in prewar Europe in 1937 and 1938, and in Honolulu, Hawaii, in 1939. Roy Edward saw the smoke rising from Lakehurst, New Jersey, in 1937, when the *Hindenburg* exploded as it was docking.

Hyperion Studio facility in the Los Angeles neighborhood of Silver Lake, circa 1930s

Left to right: Roy O. Disney, Edna Disney, unknown, Walt Disney, unknown, Kathryn Beaumont, and Roy E. Disney

My dad grew up among some of the most creative people in the world. From Frank Thomas, Ollie Johnston, and Ward Kimball at Disney Studio to James Thurber, Igor Stravinsky, and Salvador Dali, who sought to work with his Uncle Walt. Roy grew up in the golden age of animation and film.

He was also a bright and inquisitive young man. He had a pilot's license at sixteen. He also went to college at sixteen. In fact, he went to college as a very young man with a freshman class of returning war veterans from World War II, many of whom were in their midtwenties and who had seen things most of us should never have to see.

He intended to study engineering at Pomona College. This dovetailed with his love of flying. His math skills, however, were not what they would need to be. He managed to flunk calculus. And so the engineering plan was scrapped.

Roy Edward did not let that get him down. He pursued writing and English because it came naturally to him, and he graduated on time.

His first job out of college was not at the Disney Studio. He worked as a page at NBC and as a production assistant for Jack Webb on the television series *Dragnet*. When *Dragnet* ended, he applied to Disney and was hired into the editorial department where he was again exposed to the heart and soul of the filmmaking process.

He married Patricia "Patty" Daily in 1955; shortly thereafter, flying was taken off the table by his young wife. So, he took up sailing, which became his greatest passion.

Left to right: Roy E. Disney and wife Patricia (Patty) Daily at their wedding reception at the Lakeside Country Club (Toluca Lake, California), with Edna Disney, Monsignor Harry C. Meade, and Abigal Daily, the bride's mother

Roy and Patty leaving on a cruise ship for Europe on their honeymoon

Left to right: Susan, Patty, Abby, Donald Duck, Roy E.,
Roy Pat, and Tim Disney

Left to right: Tim, Abby, Susan, and Roy Pat at the Walt Disney World
property; the mound of dirt in the background is where the castle now
stands at the Magic Kingdom.

He cruised and raced around the world with his family, sailing more than one hundred thousand miles in the process.

Dad stayed at the Disney Studios as an editor. He also wrote and produced eighteen different hour-long TV nature shows and several documentaries, one of which, *Mysteries of the Deep* (1959), was nominated for an Academy Award. During that time he witnessed the birth of his four children, the death of his Uncle Walt, the opening of Walt Disney World, and the death of his father, Roy Oliver.

Roy with Norman "Stormy" Palmer, circa late 1950s

Roy in his studio office with a Moviola

He left the studio in 1977 to produce movies on his own. Over time, the Walt Disney Studios continued to drift and suffer from a lack of vision and creativity. So, in 1983 Roy Edward Disney led a group of allied investors to take over the studio and replace its management. He brought in Michael Eisner, Frank Wells (a former college classmate), and Jeffery Katzenberg. Item number one initially of the business plan for the new board members was to eliminate the animation department. But Roy E., with his extensive history and deep understanding of the core of Disney, spoke up and said, "No, I will take care of animation; it is too important to this company."

Roy, Michael Eisner, and Mickey Mouse

He led the drive to reinvigorate and modernize Disney animation. He created a nurturing environment for the animators. He helped introduce computers and computer animation to the company. He helped mold and develop story lines for the new feature films. He felt, as Walt had, that the creative talents at the studio were part of a family. He treated them as such. He travelled with the animators. He brought them into his home. He loved them, and they loved him.

Many of the new animation artists had come through the California Institute of the Arts, a school in Valencia, California, which Walt and Roy Oliver had founded and on whose board Roy Edward sat as one of the trustees. One such artist was the author of this book, Dave Bossert. He graduated from CalArts in 1983 with a degree from the Character Animation program, and came to

12

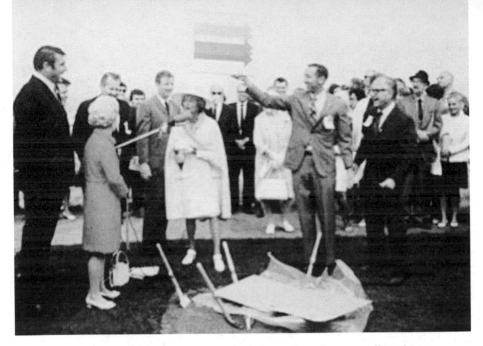

Roy, holding the colored arrows placard, at the groundbreaking of CalArts in Valencia, California, on May 3, 1969. Buzz Price is to Roy's left, while Ron Miller is on the far right of Roy, behind Lillian Disney (who's in the red coat).

the Disney Studios in early 1984. He met my father a few times early on, but began to work closely with him when Dad began to push for a remake of one of his favorite animated films that his uncle and father made: *Fantasia*.

Left to right: Steve Lavine, president of CalArts; Roy E.; and Nancy and Dave Bossert. PHOTO BY SCOTT GOLLER

Roy, with James Lavine and Mickey, backstage at Carnegie Hall for the premiere of Fantasia/2000; *December 17, 1999*

Dave Bossert and Don Hahn at the Boston Museum of Fine Arts in November 2010. PHOTO COURTESY OF NANCY HILL

They worked closely together on *Fantasia/2000*, as well as many other animated pieces, including *One by One*, *The Little Match Girl*, *Lorenzo*, and *Destino*. He also helped my dad get the True-Life Adventures films out on DVD. *Lorenzo* and *Destino* were both nominated for Academy Awards. Dave came to know my father well and often travelled with him and other animators to Florida and to Europe, where Disney had animation studios at the time.

Through those travels and projects, Dave Bossert came to know a much broader view of a complex and talented man. My father led a fascinating life and cared deeply about what he did and those he worked with. He cared most deeply about the heritage that is his family name, Disney.

In this book are stories and adventures of this multi-faceted man and his interactions with so many talented and artistic people. I hope you will enjoy their retellings as much as I have.

—Roy Patrick Disney

Roy E. and Roy Pat at the Mary Poppins *Broadway premiere in New York City*

Salvador Dali and Walt Disney

Introduction

It was in early November of 2010 that I found myself at the Onyx Hotel in Boston, Massachusetts. It was a small, quiet boutique hotel tucked away on a side street within walking distance of the Boston Garden, the arena where the Celtics and Bruins play.

I had just arrived at Logan Airport on a damp, drizzly Saturday afternoon after a very long flight from Barcelona, Spain, via Frankfurt, Germany. I was exhausted from the travel, but had a pair of tickets to see a Bruins hockey game at the Boston Garden—and since my date for the evening was my eldest daughter, Sydney, you can be sure I was going.

We were on the second leg of a journey to promote the release of the *Fantasia–Fantasia/2000* Blu-ray disc. The disc included the short film *Destino*—a collaboration between Walt Disney and Salvador Dali.

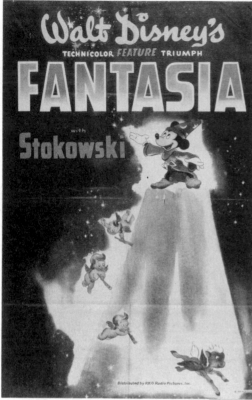

Fantasia *1940*

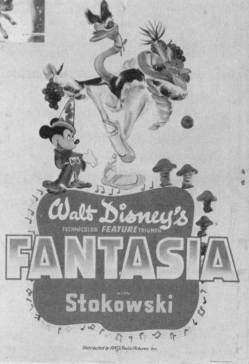

Fantasia/2000

The studio had released the *Destino* short as a bonus feature on the *Fantasia–Fantasia/2000* Blu-ray. Typically when a studio releases a new DVD or Blu-ray disc, they would schedule a series of events in a variety of locations in order to get as much press coverage as possible. This *Fantasia–Fantasia/2000* release was extra special because it contained the short film *Destino*, and a documentary about its making.

Back in 1946, Salvador Dali had an unlikely collaboration with Walt Disney on a short film that was to be called *Destino*.

Legend has it that Walt and Dali had met at a Hollywood party and immediately hit it off. They were fascinated with and admired each other; ultimately, they agreed to work together on a project. That turned out to be *Destino*—a topic of a later chapter in this book.

Although the short film was never completed by these two artists, they remained lifelong friends. They exchanged letters and visited each other when time permitted.

Now, fast-forward to late 1998, and *Destino* resurfaced while we were working on *Fantasia/2000*, which was the continuation of what Walt had referred to as his greatest achievement, *Fantasia*. This new *Fantasia* film was the brainchild of Roy and a project that he was intimately involved in from start to finish. It was a project that I would spend five years working on!

Fantasia was a packaged picture that grew out of the animated short "Sorcerer's Apprentice," which apparently cost so much to make at the time that Walt decided to do other segments and release it as a feature. That was the only way that the studio would hope to be able to make back the costs spent on the "Sorcerer's Apprentice" short.

It was Roy E. Disney who first mentioned the artwork that had been generated by Salvador Dali and Disney artist John Hench, and thought we should include some of the art in an interstitial on "the Disney that never was" for *Fantasia/2000*. In between each short animation piece in both *Fantasia* and *Fantasia/2000* is a live-action segment referred to as an interstitial. One of those segments delves into the past projects that may have been developed to a point and, for one reason or another, was shut down or shelved.

When Roy suggested that we put some of the *Destino*

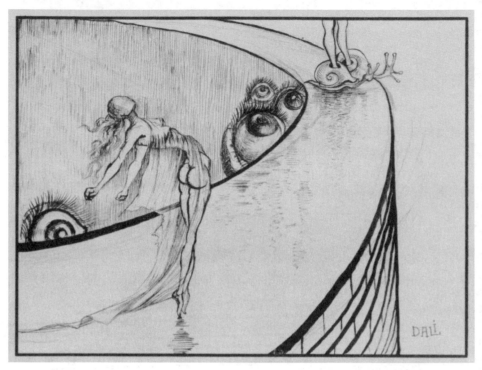

Story sketch for Disney Destino; *ink on paper by Salvador Dali, 1946*

art into that particular interstitial, it sparked a lot of interest. That suggestion ultimately planted the seed that would flourish into a group of us completing the *Destino* short in 2003! (More on *Destino* later.)

By all rights it was Roy E. who would have gone to Spain to speak about the *Destino* short and both *Fantasia* films. The original 1940 *Fantasia* was one of Roy's favorite movies that his Uncle Walt made. But sadly, Roy had passed away nearly a year before this event, and so I was asked by the studio to represent the projects at the Salvador Dali Museum and the Dali home.

At the Onyx Hotel, I met up with Don Hahn, a studio colleague and longtime friend who had actually first hired me at the Disney studio in early 1984. We had worked together on many projects over the years, and he has always been a wonderful collaborator and confidant.

Don not only produced some of the most celebrated animated films of all time—*Beauty and the Beast* and *The Lion King*—but he also directed the interstitials for *Fantasia/2000*. He is a renaissance man of sorts, as he has not only produced great films, he has written and directed

Final from the Disney short animated film Destino

other film projects and has also had a number of books published over the years.

Don had flown into Boston to help promote the Blu-ray. It was in the hotel's Ruby Room lounge that Don and I were chatting about our recent adventures and catching up. Naturally the conversation eventually drifted toward our presentation the next evening, and we started talking about *Destino*, *Fantasia*, and *Fantasia/2000*, and Roy.

There were so many stories to share about Roy. Any time you spent with him seemed like a great adventure. The guy truly led a storied life, which ultimately included being the protector and savior of the Disney empire.

Roy in cigarette smoke; caricature by John Musker

Roy, Mickey, and James Lavine onstage at the premiere of
Fantasia/2000 *at Carnegie Hall December 17, 1999*

For me personally, just being with Roy was absolutely incredible, and a story in itself! Many of those stories were hilarious; others were hair-raising, outrageous, and unbeliev-able, and some were quite poignant and touching. The best thing about it is that everyone who knew Roy had all these terrific stories, and many times you would hear a new one that you hadn't known about before.

I had worked closely with Roy on numerous projects during the last decades of his life. We had had some great experiences and many journeys together, from travelling aboard his private jet to witnessing some veterinary dentis-try to lending him some money; seriously I lent a billionaire a few bucks.

It was in the Ruby Room lounge at the Onyx Hotel in Boston that Don Hahn said to me, "You know, you ought to write a book about Roy!" He thought that I had so many great stories that it might be worth documenting them in a book—putting many of those stories in print for others to enjoy, and at the same time paying homage to the man who touched so many of us.

I thought about that conversation a lot over the next several months. It was almost haunting in the way it kept resurfacing in my mind.

Don had already published a number of books himself, so I took his suggestion seriously.

It did seem like a daunting task to write a book though; where would I start, what exactly would I write about, and how much should I reveal? It would need to be authentic, down to earth like Roy was. It needed to be revealing but at the same time respectful and considerate. Not some snarky tell-all, but a more genuine personal account of Roy: stories and observations.

It's not like there are any terrible secrets or anything inappropriate, but we all have conversations about situations or individuals that we would not want to put into print or have published. I am someone that is very respectful of that.

My thought was to create a collection of memories: wonderful, funny, and insightful recollections of Roy that provide a window of sorts into the world of Roy E. Disney that few would ever have the pleasure to experience. It would paint a portrait, in words and pictures, of a man who touched the lives of so many and truly accomplished so much on his own.

It was not a task that I was considering lightly, and there were far more questions than I had answers to. But the one aim I had as my guiding light was to put together a book that truly celebrated Roy, a book that would be a personal thank-you from me for all the great projects and incredible times that I had with him over the years. Without getting too schmaltzy, it would be a deeply personal note of appreciation and affection.

So, I bought a book on how to write a book. I know that sounds amusing, but it was a great way to get some insight into the process of authoring a book, and it actually pointed

Roy in his Team Disney office at the main studio lot in Burbank

me in the right direction. It gave me the basics, a road map to what I needed to do to get this book project off the ground.

I offer this background so that you, the reader, know that this project has been a personal mission of mine and a heartfelt thank-you to Roy.

Don was kind enough to put me in touch with Wendy Lefkon at Disney Publishing Worldwide. Though we knew many of the same people, our paths had never actually crossed. We agreed to meet up while I was on a business trip in New York.

At some point prior to that lunch meeting with Wendy in New York, I decided that if I were to write this book I had to ask some of Roy's family members for permission to do it in the first place. If they weren't amenable to it, then the project would have died on the vine, because I would not be doing it if there was any resistance. I was also hopeful in getting some assistance as well!!

I talked to Roy's eldest son, Roy Patrick Disney, over a lunch in the studio commissary and asked him what he thought about me writing a book about his father. I explained what my thinking was about writing the book and the conversations that I had had with Don Hahn. My thought was that if Roy E.'s eldest son was okay with it then that was a very good start!

Roy Patrick Disney, known to many as Roy Pat, thought it was a great idea and a wonderful way to honor his father. He asked some good probing questions to get a better

Front row (left to right): Tim, Abby, Susan, and Roy Pat; back row (left to right): Roy O., Edna, Patty, and Roy E. in Washington, D.C., March 1969, for the presentation of the Walt Disney Commemorative Medal

sense of what I wanted to accomplish with the book; it all boiled down to celebrating his father. With that understanding, Roy Pat approved right away and even agreed to write the foreword to this book.

I also reached out to Roy E.'s widow, Leslie DeMeuse Disney, and spoke with her as well. It was important to have Leslie's approval; she was Roy E.'s second wife and was the person who spent the last years of Roy's life by his side, loving and caring for him.

Leslie and I spoke at length about the book project and what I would be writing about. She wanted to make sure that it was going to be sensitive to their personal lives and to the entire family.

Roy and his first wife, Patty, had divorced, and he eventually got married to Leslie. Both Patty and Leslie were and are terrific women. Throughout this book there are stories that will include them as they were the women who shared Roy's life. He loved them both dearly!

To put Leslie's mind at ease, I told her that I had never seen Roy happier than when they were together, and it was an important part of his story. Toward the end of the conversation, Leslie agreed that it would be a good project, and she said she knew that I cared about Roy E. and wanted to celebrate him. She understood I wasn't going to write anything that would in any way besmirch his memory.

With Roy Pat and Leslie comfortable, I headed for New York. There certainly was no shortage of things to talk about over lunch. Wendy and I hit it off so well and had so many great friends in common, as well as a bunch of great Roy stories to trade, it was hard to believe that we had not met before this meeting. There was no question in my mind at the end of lunch that I had gained a supporter in writing this book project on Roy E.

I was equally delighted when I received an e-mail from Wendy telling me, "I got the group to sign off on the book." My response was one of sheer joy and I responded, "I am JUMPING UP AND DOWN IN MY office!!!!! This is awesome news and I cannot thank you enough for your support and belief in this project. WE ARE GOING TO MAKE ROY E. PROUD!!"

To say that I was excited about getting the go-ahead to write this book would be an understatement. I mean, when you think about it, how lucky is it to have spent enough time with someone as great as Roy and be able to write a book about it.

Now it was time to get down to it and put in writing, all of these great stories and really honor Roy's memory with a tribute that would be reasonably in-depth, funny, thoughtful, respectful, and, above all, faithful to his memory.

By no means was or is this book intended to be an in-depth biography of Roy Edward Disney's life. That needs to be left to someone with a much greater skill-set, a biographer, as Roy was a multifaceted man who led a complex and storied life.

He had many sides to that life, which was best described and delineated in the program that a group of us helped to put together for his life celebration in January of 2010. Roy was a family man, businessman/Hollywood scion, sailor, filmmaker, and the leader of Disney Animation.

I am basically concentrating on Roy E. Disney the leader of Disney Animation and all the exploits that I and many others had from around the early 1990s through his

passing in late 2009. I will also be touching on the sailing, not only because it was a passion of Roy's, but because there was some overlap on that topic with Roy and me.

During that period, I found myself working mostly on projects that were spearheaded and executive produced by Roy E. Disney; they're projects that continued to build on and/or document the Disney Animation legacy. Films like *Fantasia/2000, Destino, One by One, The Little Match Girl*, and *Lorenzo*, were our primary focus, as was the releasing of the True-Life Adventures films on DVD.

These were all projects that had special meaning to many of us who worked on them for a variety of reasons. But they were especially noteworthy because they were all executive produced by Roy, and he was intimately involved with each and every one.

You will find in this book many of my own personal memories, stories, and artifacts that I collected along the way. These are bits and pieces that I squirreled away in binders and envelopes that were filled with nearly three decades of adventures at Walt Disney Animation Studios and with Roy.

All of these mementoes and stories are being shared, many for the first time, so that you will have a better sense of who this man we called simply "Roy" was, and the fact that he was an extraordinary individual wrapped up as an ordinary man. He bristled at being called Mr. Disney and was on a first-name basis with everyone who knew him.

There are also stories sprinkled through this book by a number of friends and colleagues who knew Roy and were gracious enough to share those moments in these pages as well.

Roy with Snow White and Dopey at Disney California Adventure

Roy used to poke fun at me because I always had a disposable camera handy (before the era of cell phone cameras), and some of those pictures are throughout this book. He also wrote many handwritten notes, some of which you'll find in these pages.

Ken Moore, a Disney projectionist, was celebrating an anniversary with the company at a theater Roy happened to be doing a presentation at on the True-Life Adventures series, and received as a gift from him the set of DVDs he is holding.

They all hold special memories of a man I often referred to as "the Boss." He was, in fact, to me the boss because his family name was on the front door at the studio in Burbank and at all things Disney.

Roy cared deeply about the company and the employees that were in the trenches daily creating incomparable guest experiences. There was never a hesitation on his part to agree to a photo with a cast member, colleague, guest, or fan. He understood all too well that such things meant something, meant a lot to those who were asking. He was always accommodating and gracious about such things.

Roy Edward Disney passed away on Wednesday, December 16, 2009, at 10:30 A.M., and on that day the world lost a true titan: the last of a Hollywood breed. Those of us who had the privilege to know him lost a friend, colleague, and a boss. He was a man who led an amazing life and had a profound impact on all who had the honor and pleasure to know and be associated with him.

I received the sad news while on the historic Stage A at Capitol Records in Hollywood. I was there with a twenty-eight-piece orchestra rerecording the masterful scores by Oliver Wallace, Frank Churchill, and others for several classic Mickey, Donald, and Goofy cartoons. This was part of a project called Have-A-Laugh. In hindsight, it was somewhat apropos to be in the middle of such classic Disney Animation when receiving the heartbreaking news of Roy's passing.

The *Los Angeles Times* obituary that ran the next day noted:

As chairman of Disney animation, Disney helped guide the studio to a new golden age of animation with an unprecedented string of artistic and box-office successes that included *The Little Mermaid*, *Beauty and the Beast*, *Aladdin*, and *The Lion King*. He was executive producer of *Fantasia/2000*, the sequel to the 1940 Disney classic, and the 2004 Oscar-nominated *Destino*, based on the 1946 collaboration between Walt Disney and Spanish painter Salvador Dali.

Roy E. Disney with Fantasia/2000 *maquettes*

It was a true honor and privilege to have known Roy, to have travelled with him over the years, and to have spent time with him. He is sorely missed, and I think about him every day when I walk into the Roy E. Disney Animation Building in Burbank, California, where my office is.

I hope that you will enjoy this book and all the stories, photos, and artifacts related to Roy. It is meant to be a celebration of Roy and a chance for you, the reader, to get a glimpse into the looking glass, an opportunity to see why he was so loved and revered at the company. More importantly, I truly hope that you will get a much better understanding of who he was and what he stood for when it came to the wonderful world of Disney.

Roy eating a hot dog at Costco; he loved hot dogs and shopping at Costco!

Chapter 1
Wealth, Value, and Quality

"There by the grace of God
walks the richest man in the trailer park!"

—George Scribner, director of *Oliver & Company*
and *The Prince and the Pauper,* commenting
on Roy E. Disney crossing the studio parking lot.

Roy E. Disney was a billionaire at one point in his life. In 2005, *Forbes* magazine listed him as having a net worth of $1.2 billion. That's an awful lot of money, but Roy came across more like a working stiff. In fact, most people are shocked when I tell them that he used to shop at the Burbank Costco, and he ate at the Toluca Lake Taco Bell from time to time.

Some years ago, someone posted a sighting of Roy at that Taco Bell, and the post even described what he ordered. Someone at the studio saw it online and forwarded it to Roy. He readily admitted that he had eaten at that Taco Bell, with an impish smile, but he commented that the person who posted the comments got his meal description all wrong.

Stanley Gold, Roy's business partner

According to Roy's longtime business partner Stanley Gold, "He didn't know how much money he had. He never knew how much money he had. That was actually my job. He didn't care about money."

Stanley recalls how Roy was always focused on a quest for quality and not the expenses it entailed.

We were going to build a new building on the northwest corner of Lakeside and Barham; it was the first new building in Burbank subject to a new law that required owners to install a work of public art to help beautify the city. Our obligation was to spend something like $25,000 on that art. So, we design the building, and we put in some kind of art or at least what the designer put in was some kind of light show as the artwork. And I showed it to Roy, and he says, "It's horrible." I said, "What's horrible?

Cameraman statue on the corner of West Lakeside Drive and Olive Avenue in Burbank

The building?" "No, no, the building is fine, the piece of art." He said, "I'll do it." I said, okay. Your building, your money. You'll do it. He commissioned an Italian artist who had done a lot of statuary work in the parks.

Stanley went on to say:

He built this wonderful statue of an old-time cameraman. It's sort of an entrance to Burbank. It's fabulous, and it cost us $250,000 when our obligation was only $25,000. And I said to him, you know you're like $225,000 over budget. He said, "But it's nice. It's good. It's quality. I'm proud to own it, and the building behind it. And it's a contribution to the city." That was his attitude. He didn't know how much it cost. It's typical of Roy. He would like to do it right, and he didn't know, nor did he care how much it cost.

When we were working on *Fantasia/2000*, Roy and his first wife, Patty, had travelled to the family home in Ireland for a couple of months one summer. While over there, Roy was fond of tooling around in his vintage Mini Cooper. Not like one of the newer Mini Coopers (the company is now owned by BMW), but an older, original model.

In Ireland you drive on the left side of the road. So, if you are not used to driving on the opposite side of the road it is easy, especially out in the middle of nowhere, to drift onto the wrong, or more familiar, side.

Roy and Patty Disney

*Roy signing True-Life Adventures DVDs at the Studio Store
on the Disney Studios lot in Burbank*

While driving on a desolate road, Roy had in fact drifted over into the more familiar right lane of the road and wound up getting into a serious accident with another car. He broke his left leg rather severely, which required a cast and a wheelchair for weeks.

Once he returned home to Southern California for medical treatment, he came by the studio in his wheelchair a number of times for screenings and updates.

One day we were expecting him for a screening, and he walked in with the help of a cane to everyone's delight. We were all happy to see him out of the wheelchair and on the road to a full recovery and broke into a raucous applause.

Roy just smiled and he held up the cane he was using horizontally with both hands and said, "It's $19.99 at Savon!" Savon was a local drugstore chain in Southern California that he frequented.

These stories might be unusual or out of the ordinary for the rich and famous, but not for Roy. These were actually typical of Roy; he was not pretentious, nor did he ever feel going into any of these stores was beneath him in any way.

On one trip to Dublin, we hosted several cocktail receptions for a group of animation artists. We had pinned artwork around the room to show off a number of upcoming projects. When we were done, we were all starving and wanted to go to dinner but had to take the art down. Roy, without hesitation or being asked, jumped in and helped us unpin that artwork so that we could all go out to dinner.

Roy was as comfortable talking to the security guard at the Animation Building as he was chatting with European royalty or a U.S. president. He was as fine with waiting in the queue for the Walt Disney World Monorail as he was having a driver take him around the parks.

Okay, he did have a penchant for Ferraris, racing sloops, and planes. For many of us who knew Roy well, his plane is a rich source of great stories. In fact there is an entire chapter devoted to "Air Roy."

One night I found myself waiting for Roy outside a small restaurant in Hollywood. It was a little, nondescript place on a side street, and I figured by waiting outside it would be easier for him to find it. I was looking for Roy's red Ferrari to come tooling around the corner and instead came this red Mini Cooper. Roy was behind the wheel. I did a double take.

When I walked up to the car, a bit dumbstruck, I asked him why he was driving a Mini. He said with the crazy gas prices it was costing him a small fortune every time he went anywhere in the Ferrari, so he got this Mini to save on gas. He may not have known exactly how much money he had at any given time but he knew the value of a dollar.

In 2007 Roy and I set out on a trip to promote the True-Life Adventures DVD collection we had just completed. It was a series of eight discs packaged into four DVD boxes. The trip took us from Los Angeles to Orlando, then on to New York, and then finally home to Burbank. As we were planning the trip, Roy asked if we could fly JetBlue because it flew in and out of the Bob Hope Airport in Burbank.

It was a request that I had to get cleared because JetBlue was not an approved airline for Disney company travel. The executive who okayed this request practically fell out of his chair when we asked if we could fly JetBlue. After all, Roy could fly first class or on the private jet if he wanted to.

Naturally, the request was approved, but as it turned out

Roy sitting with the statue of his father, Roy O. Disney,
at Disney World Resort, Orlando, Florida

we could only get the last leg of the trip from New York's JFK Airport to Burbank on JetBlue.

While we were at Walt Disney World we stayed at the Grand Floridian Resort, and Roy stayed in the "Roy O. Disney" suite named for his father. The Roy O. Disney suite is available to any guests but is usually the room that Roy stayed in while on the Florida property. He enjoyed it because it had many framed family photos as part of the decor.

At Disney's Animal Kingdom, Roy was scheduled to speak on a series of live satellite feeds to a variety of morning talk shows across the country. It was wonderful to have Roy in the middle of the park that he so dearly loved.

Once we were finished with all the interviews and promotional work that needed to be done, we'd fly to New York the following morning. As we checked out of the hotel a bellman helped us with our bags and we each gave him a few dollars as a tip.

We landed on time at JFK Airport in New York. Roy owned an apartment in New York City, and when we were planning the trip he had invited me to stay at his place instead of a hotel. It was a very gracious gesture and one that I took him up on without hesitation.

Once the car reached his apartment, we went in, and Roy told me to take one of the bedrooms down the hall, gesturing to his left. I dutifully went down the hall and put my bags down, took a look around, and went back out into the living room.

It was there that I saw Roy just standing there looking down at his hands and checking his pockets a few times. He had a very puzzled look on his face and was clearly confused by something that happened.

I said, "What's the matter?"

Roy responded by saying that he had lost some money.

I said, "What do you mean you lost some money?" as if there was a stock market crash and he lost some serious coin. No, he said that he had had a few hundred dollars and now had only a few dollars; he lost all the cash that he had on him.

After double-checking his pockets a few more times,

*Roy speaking about the True-Life Adventures DVD series
to cast members at Disney's Animal Kingdom*

I suggested that we just hit an ATM before dinner so he had some pocket money.

Roy looked up at me, somewhat wide-eyed, and said he didn't have an ATM card. I looked at him and said, "Seriously?" with a smile on my face. "Dude, it's the twenty-first century, everybody has an ATM card; how can you not have one?" He verified that he did not have an ATM card, so I told him I had mine and would be happy to get some money to lend him.

He looked at me a bit chagrined and asked me if I was sure that would be all right; I laughed and told him, yeah, I not only know where you work but also where you live!

The next morning I got up early and went out for a walk before Roy was up. While I was out, I stopped by an ATM and withdrew some money for Roy.

When I got back to the apartment Roy was up. He was wearing a blue bathrobe, his hair was disheveled, and he was slumped in a cushioned armchair watching ABC's *Good Morning America*—always the company man.

I let him know I had gotten some cash from the ATM on the corner and asked him if a $100 would do for now or if he needed more. He agreed that a $100 would be fine.

So, with a smile I asked him to put his hand out level and flat. He raised an eyebrow and complied as I counted out $100 in twenties into the palm of his hand. I told him with a big smile not to spend it all in one place.

After we laughed about it, he thanked me and assured me that I would get the hundred bucks back once we got back to Burbank.

But losing the money certainly did bug Roy during our

trip. He brought it up several times over the next few days. It was really gnawing at him.

Once we were done with our business in New York, we headed to the JetBlue terminal at JFK for our return flight to Burbank. At the gate I bought us some sandwiches and chips for the flight home. Picture it: I'm sitting with Roy E. Disney on a no-frills JetBlue flight, and we're eating sandwiches. Not bad for a kid from Massapequa, New York.

At one point Roy looked at me and said, "I just don't know what happened to that money!" I made a wisecrack that maybe he was having a senior moment and if he was starting to forget things that maybe I better write out an IOU for the money I lent him.

And with that, I promptly wrote on the back of a JetBlue cocktail napkin, ROY OWES DAVE $100. Roy smiled and reached over and scribbled his first name to it and we had a laugh.

A few weeks after we returned home, Roy told me that

IOU for $100 on JetBlue cocktail napkin; a priceless keepsake!

he received a letter from the bellman at the Grand Floridian Resort at Walt Disney World with "lost" money. It turns out that when he tipped the bellman, Roy had inadvertently handed the man several hundred dollars instead of the two bucks that he was planning on giving the gentleman. The bellman returned it to Roy with a letter saying that he figured it was a mistake and wanted Roy to have the money back.

Roy actually wrote the gentleman back and sent a nice tip along with his note. The mystery was solved.

As for me, did I get my $100 back? Well, that is the question everyone has asked me when I tell this story. The fact is Roy told me that he would have his secretary, Monica Ellsbury, return the $100 to me right away when we had returned to Los Angeles.

Monica even phoned me and said she had the money at Roy's office and that I could drop by anytime to pick it up. I never did go and pick up that money for several reasons.

First, Roy had always been generous to me. It was amazing that he had invited me to stay at his place in New York City during that trip. And second, I get to keep my signed IOU on a JetBlue napkin as a memento of the trip. Priceless!

Roy and Patty looking at the donor wall at CalArts

Chapter 2
Philanthropy and Generosity

"It's not hard to make decisions
when you know what your values are."

—Roy E. Disney

The Roy E. Disney family has been generous with their philanthropy over the years. Roy used to tell me how the family would gather together as a group annually to discuss what organizations they would be making donations to and how much they would be distributing each year.

Roy made a personal $400,000 donation each year to the California Institute of the Arts in Valencia, California. The institute, known as CalArts, which was the brainchild of Walt Disney in the early 1960s, is an art college focusing on five performing and visual arts under one roof: theater, music, art, design, and film. The school has since added a sixth department called Critical Studies, comprised of various writing programs.

In addition to CalArts being the number one art school in the country according to a survey by *Newsweek/Daily*

Top row (left to right): Joe Lanzisero, Darrell Van Citters, Brett Thompson,
John Lasseter, Leslie Margolin, Mike Cedeno, Paul Nowak, Nancy Beiman
Seated or leaning on model stand: Jerry Rees, Bruce Morris,
instructor Elmer Plummer, Brad Bird, Doug Lefler
In front, seated: Harry Sabin and John Musker
PHOTO © HARRY SABIN

Beast in 2011, it is also a training ground for new animation artists. The film school at CalArts is known the world over for its Character Animation program, originally organized by a number of Disney artists when they retired from the studio. There were Disney Legends, such as Jack Hannah, T. Hee, Elmer Plummer, and Ken Anderson, all teaching at the school in the late 1970s and early 1980s.

That Character Animation program at CalArts turned out a who's who of contemporary Disney and Pixar animation artists and directors: John Musker, Brad Bird, John Lasseter, Tim Burton, and many other successful and accomplished filmmakers.

It was very special to Roy—not only because it was conceived by his Uncle Walt but also because the vision was continued by Roy's father after Walt's death. It was also the training ground—the animation boot camp for each new generation of Disney artists.

Many of those artists helped to reignite a renaissance in animation in the late 1980s and 1990s, with films like *The Little Mermaid*, *Beauty and the Beast*, *The Lion King*, *Toy Story*, *The Nightmare Before Christmas*, and many others.

Roy E. was there from the beginning when they broke ground for the school in Valencia, and he remained a trustee of the institute until his death.

In late 1999, I was contacted by then vice president of development for CalArts, Jeff James. He asked if I would be interested in helping to put together an event celebrating the thirtieth anniversary of the school. I had graduated from CalArts in 1983, and Jeff was anxious to get some alumni more involved with CalArts and promised it would not take up a lot of time. (Don't ever fall for that line.)

Our small committee put together a celebration that included a sit-down dinner for a thousand people prepared by noted celebrity chef John Sedlar, entertainment, and a fireworks display. And the honorary chairpersons for the event were Roy and Patty Disney.

It's always bothered me when people organizing an event

Roy and Patty Disney at the CalArts commencement

choose to honor someone because they have lots of friends who would buy tables. When members of the committee asked me to ask Roy to buy a table for the event I said no way! I told them that my wife, Nancy, and I were buying a table, and that we would invite Roy and Patty to be our guests, but there was no way we would be asking them for money. I mean Roy, Patty, and the entire family have been incredibly generous to CalArts for as long as it has been in existence, so the least we could do was be respectful of that.

I invited Roy and Patty to attend as guests of my wife, Nancy, and me. I told him what was being planned, and that we wanted to honor both he and Patty by making them

Los Angeles Mayor Antonio Villaraigosa and Steve Lavine present Roy with the REDCAT Award designed by Frank Gehry and produced by Tiffany at the REDCAT gala in 2007

Roy receives an honorary Doctor of Arts degree from CalArts in 2003.
PHOTO BY SCOTT GROLLER

honorary alumni of the institute. Roy happily accepted and expressed his view that the future of CalArts would be with its alumni. He went on to say that anything he could do to help out with alumni events he'd be happy to do, and I told him that just showing up at the events would be great.

The other reason why I never wanted to ask Roy for money was a very valuable lesson I learned while attending CalArts. There are two kinds of debts in life. There is the debt that one incurs with credit cards, mortgages, and loans. It is a debt that will eventually be paid off over time; it's a personal responsibility to make good on your word and return the money you borrowed.

The other kind of debt is one of gratitude. It is a gratefulness and recognition that allows you to thank someone who has done something selfless to help you. Gratitude is that appreciation and acknowledgment that you show anyone for something that they have done to help you. This is the kind of debt that is not repayable over time. It is not a liability; there is no balance due or money owed; you can only chip away at a debt of gratitude over your lifetime. Even when that person is gone, you can still pay it forward by helping others.

I was only able to attend CalArts on a Disney scholarship, and, without that scholarship, it would have been nearly impossible for me to attain my degree. So for me the scholarship was more than just a resource to finish school, it was the means to building a wonderful and fulfilling career: a multidecades-long association with The Walt Disney Company.

So, when I started working at the Disney Studios, it was

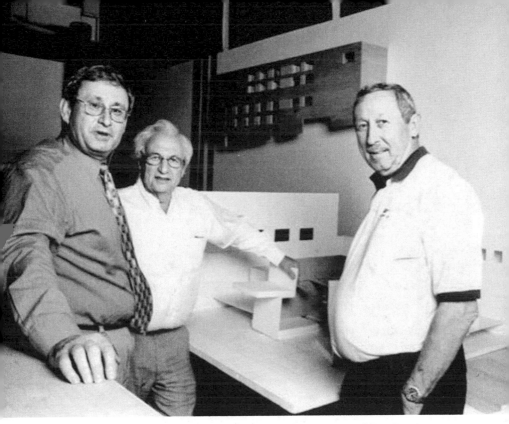

Steven Lavine, president of CalArts, Frank Gehry, and Roy Disney review model of REDCAT Theater at Disney Concert Hall

always my intention to go above and beyond; to come in every day and give *150 percent*. It was my way of chipping away at that debt.

Without ever telling him my reasons, when I got to know Roy, I focused on doing whatever I could to help him and never expected anything in return. Outside of attending the CalArts Alumni Association events or helping out CalArts in that way, I never asked him for anything. I only ever wanted to assist him in completing whatever project he was interested in doing at Disney Animation.

During the years I knew Roy he frequently did things for

John Lasseter, Roy, and Thomas Schumacher at the Mary Poppins *Broadway premiere*

others that he didn't have to or need to do. He understood that a simple word to someone or a phone call could make a difference in someone's life.

John Lasseter in his own words:

Roy was just was such a generous, great man. My wife, Nancy, and I were on a publicity tour for Toy Story 2 *and we went for the first time to Ireland. At the time, Trish Long was I think the marketing and publicity head for Ireland; now she's the country head. Roy and Trish were friends 'cause Roy had his place in County Cork. And so Roy got word that Nancy and I were coming to Ireland.*

And so he picked up the phone, called Trish, and says I want John and Nancy to come visit Patty and I. We're at the house, so of course Trish makes an arrangement. After I did the publicity in Dublin and saw Dublin, she put us on a train to Cork.

When we arrived in Cork City we walk off the train with our bags and there are Roy and Patty meeting us. We climb into their car and, and Roy drives us to their house. We pull up to their house and it's a castle, right. But he was very clear to say it's not a castle. It's a castle-ized manor house. It was like the hip thing to do back I don't know in the 1700s or something like that.

The English who had these big manor houses, they would then remodel them to look like castles. You know, with all the stonework and stuff like that. So it looked a lot like a castle to us. But he was very clear to say it wasn't.

The tulips were in bloom and their garden was spectacular. And I remember one of my favorite things was they had this little path. And you walked around, it was like a spiral, and it just went up to the top of this hill on the spiral. And then just there you got to the top and there was a place, a little place to stand and then you walked back down.

And it was just the cleverest kind of cartoony-est thing. It was so much fun.

But Patty and Nancy, my wife, Nancy, just hit it off. And they started talking about sort of the origins of the family and how they just got into the genealogy.

And the girls were just chatting in the kitchen, just talking about this, looking at maps, talking. Roy's just sitting there, you know, looking at 'em; he just looks over at me and says, "Let's go." He's like they're gonna be at this for hours, let's go. So we climbed in his little Mini and we took off. And we drove for arguably two hours, just the two of us. He drove around, it was after his accident, and he showed me exactly where the accident happened. And why it happened and stuff.

We stopped and went for a walk around this true old castle. And it was just me and him. We went to a pub and it was just so special for me that day. Just to have such a long time driving around Ireland completely on my own with Roy. His words, the quiet words of wisdom that day, were just so special.

Peter Schneider, the former president of Disney Animation, remarked, "Roy didn't manage his life, the company, his power, his position. He didn't do any of that for personal good. He did it all because he was fundamentally passionate about animation."

Typical of story meetings, the artists would toss quick cartoons
back and forth at each other as in this one from the film
Oliver & Company *where Roy was attending story meetings.*
Sketch by Pete Young, who passed away in 1985

George Scribner, who directed *Oliver & Company, The Prince and the Pauper*, and numerous Disney Imagineering projects, benefitted enormously from Roy's kindness. George attributes his promotion to director on *Oliver & Company* to Roy's quiet, behind-the-scenes recommendation.

George Scribner in his own words:

I'm an animation director because of Roy Disney.
I have no idea where I'd be now if it weren't for him.
For that I will always be grateful to him.
In 1985 I was a story person on an animated

Roy with George Scribner

feature we were going to do, based on Oliver Twist.
We had just begun to work on the story when we
were told that Roy wanted to join our story sessions.
We freaked. Roy? Were they joking? Were we in
trouble and he was coming to fire people?

First we got rid of all those sketches trashing the
studio or ourselves (of course) or him (he was great
fun to caricature). We vacuumed and waxed the
furniture. The room looked great when the big day
arrived. Roy showed up and let it be known he was
just going to be another story guy. Relax. He just
wanted to help out, that's all. It was the first feature

under his watch, and I think he always thought of himself as a story guy and wanted to try his hand.

Well, for about six months he came every day. He would sit in the corner of our tiny little cinder block story room, smoking furiously, nodding, willing to say really stupid things (the mark of a great story guy) and throwing out ideas with the rest of us.

I'd never met anyone like him. You just never felt he was "Roy Disney." He was just this funny, quick-witted, laid back guy named Roy. I'd never met anyone so high in a company who just didn't seem to care about his position at all. It took some getting used to. And by the way, he did turn out to have very good story sense. Thank goodness he couldn't draw or we would all been fired. He could have done it alone.

About a month after our story session with Roy ended, I was named a director on Oliver & Company, *now a full-length animated feature. My boss told me that Roy was the one who recommended me. I was overwhelmed and the next time I saw him I thanked him profusely. He told me to be quiet and quit being such a kiss ass. Ah, so Roy. He told me I'd earned it and to try and live up to it. I've tried.*

He was relentlessly mischievous. He knew I hated to fly so he gleefully sent me a video of him flying with the Blue Angels just to torture me. I sent him back some fake vomit, and he sent it back with a note saying I was a huge wussy. He was right.

It was Roy who, in 1994, kept me from leaving the studio and interceded on my behalf after I made some singularly stupid career decisions. I was very close to being let go, and he did some things for me I will never forget. So, Roy, twenty years later, I'm still here at Disney, thank you. He once told me during this very strange time in my career to learn to take work seriously, but not myself. I never forgot this. It seems obvious, but, coming from him, it just stayed with me.

I really miss him. I owe him everything.

George's story was typical of how Roy would do something for someone and it would have this profound effect on the person, a ripple effect through that person's life. It is an amazing thing to see how a simple act of kindness to a colleague or even someone you don't even know can resonate and make a deep impact.

Stanley Gold in his own words:

Roy was willing to help people in lots of ways. Whether it was just somebody coming into his office, giving him career advice, or trying to help him find a job. Or if he didn't know how to help him, he'd call me and he'd say, "Do we know anybody that can

Roy had graciously agreed to be the honorary chair for the inaugural TPC/West Ranch Art & Wine Gala to benefit the arts in the Santa Clarita Valley where CalArts is located in California. He was happy to lend his name to an event that benefitted the arts and CalArts in particular. Pictured left to right: Gala cochairs Leslie Jacobs, Dave Bossert, and Guy LeLarge with Roy in front of the Hyperion Bungalow at the Walt Disney Studios.

help somebody?" He thought that giving a person a lift up was an important thing. And again, he didn't do it so much consciously. It was part of who he was. It wasn't because he was trying to impress the individual or throw his weight around as a studio exec. It was because it was his second nature to help, it was ingrained in him. He had very defined rules about right and wrong. They were clear lines for him.

Many times over the years, because Roy was perceived as down to earth and approachable, he would often be invited to gatherings at the Animation Building or other locales. These were parties or get-togethers that you might have thought were just for the rank and file; but if Roy got an invite, he would attend if he could.

For instance, when Joe Grant turned ninety-five, there was a birthday party thrown for him at the Disney Animation Studios building in Burbank. Roy wouldn't have missed that for the world. He had known Joe for decades.

At another special event that Roy had RSVP'd "no" to, he surprised everyone by showing up.

Howard Green (veteran studio publicity executive) in his own words:

The memory for me that best reflects Roy's true character and sense of loyalty involved my New

Howard Green and Roy on Howard and Steinunn's wedding day

Year's Eve wedding on January 31, 2008. Roy and his wife, Leslie, had RSVP'd that they wouldn't be able to attend because of a scheduled ocean voyage in preparation for a new documentary film they were working on. My bride-to-be, Steinunn, who had enjoyed the company of Roy and Leslie on several memorable occasions, and I were disappointed but completely understood.

When the day of our wedding arrived, Roy and Leslie surprised us with their presence, and it meant the world to us. They had a great time mingling with other Disney colleagues and a few Legends, and were among the last to leave. It wasn't until a few weeks

later that Roy told me he had been diagnosed with
stomach cancer the week before the wedding, and
it had altered his travel plans. He added that
he was so glad to have been able to attend the
wedding, and how excited he was to surprise us. Less
than a year later, our friend Roy lost his valiant fight,
despite the bravest and most determined desire to
live I have ever seen. Every morning when I enter
the Roy E. Disney Animation Building (posthumously
renamed in his honor), I think of my friend, the
wonderful adventures we had together, and the
lasting impact that he will always have on the art
form and studio that he loved.

One of Roy's favorite projects, *Fantasia/2000*, was a film that a group of us worked on for more than five years. Toward the end of 1999, shortly before the film premiered, I received a letter from the Dale Chihuly Studio in the Seattle area, stating that a box was being shipped to my home.

Dale Chihuly is one of the preeminent glass artists in the world today, and you can see his work in countless museum collections and public spaces. A couple of the most striking pieces are hanging from the ceiling in the reception area of the Bellagio Hotel in Las Vegas or in the lobby atrium of some of the Disney cruise ships.

I didn't give it much thought. It wasn't until the large box arrived at my home that I realized that Roy had sent me an original Dale Chihuly glass sculpture as a thank-you. It came replete with a black base that had an engraved plaque

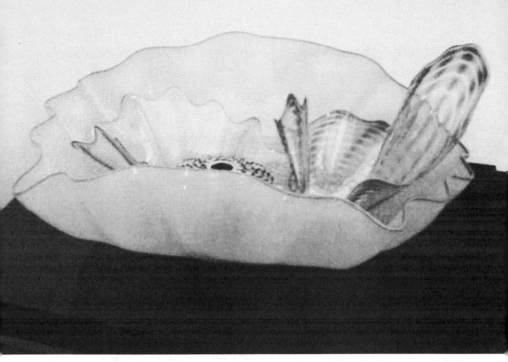

Dale Chihuly glass sculpture, a gift from Roy when we finished Fantasia/2000

Dale Chihuly glass sculpture-base plaque

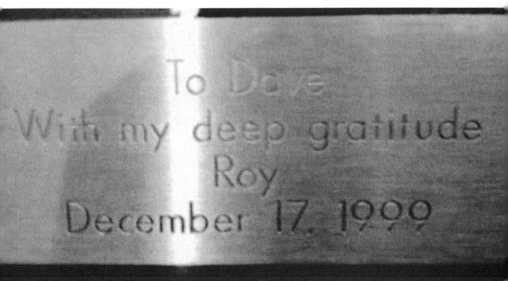

that simply read, TO DAVE, WITH MY DEEP GRATITUDE, ROY, DECEMBER 17, 1999.

Roy had also sent similar glass sculptures to the directors and producer of *Fantasia/2000* as well. In all, he sent about a dozen of these gifts to those of us who helped realize the continuation of the *Fantasia* vision.

Sailing provided Roy another opportunity to mix his passion with his generosity. Robbie Haines, the project manager for Roy's racing sloop *Pyewacket*, recalls Roy saying, "This sport has given me so much pleasure over the years that I just want to do something." Robbie responded by suggesting that "there's no better way than to give something back in the way of junior sailing. And Roy loved that."

So every year he would give a large donation to the California International Sailing Association, which promotes junior sailing in Southern California. Haines went on to say, "Roy just loved supporting that. And he did it for years and everybody appreciated it in the sailing world. Not only in this country but even worldwide; it even spread over to Ireland." Roy and Patty had a "castle" in Ireland for a time. A local Irish yacht club, Haines recalled, "approached him to do something for their junior program, which he did. He was just so darn generous. And he touched so many kids' lives in this country for so many years that they just worshipped him."

California International Sailing Association (CISA) crest

Patty Disney at CalArts commencement looking on as Roy speaks

Chapter 3
The Prom Queen Syndrome

When I was first getting to know Roy, I sensed a man that was both honored to have the name Disney and at the same time somewhat burdened by it. It was a great responsibility to look after the family legacy.

Many people would just stiffen up around Roy and treat him with the utmost respect and reverence; like royalty he was put up on a pedestal—which can be a lonely place.

It wasn't a place Roy was comfortable. He was interested, inquisitive, and could chat it up with just about anyone. He was well read and could have a conversation on any subject, although he probably loved talking about sailing most.

People generally assumed that Roy was very busy. They wouldn't even think of asking him to lunch or dinner because they figured he was booked up, that because he was a Disney, his schedule must be packed.

I learned early on in my relationship with him that it wasn't true at all. I dubbed it the Prom Queen Syndrome—everyone thinks that the Prom Queen has a date, but in reality, she doesn't; no one has asked because they all thought she already had a date.

In 1995, we were on a trip to London, where we hosted a cocktail reception for artists from the local UK animation community. London has always been a hotbed of activity in animation, and we were looking for some artists to work on *Fantasia/2000*. We certainly found some terrific talent.

We were staying at the Four Seasons in the heart of London, walking distance to Buckingham Palace. It was a beautiful hotel and a perfect location to host a gathering in one of the ballrooms.

Our Fantasia team had brought copies of various artwork representing some of the visual development that was in process for the film. These pieces were a very good representation of a variety of sequences that were in production at the time and were selected to inspire and excite some of the perspective artists that would attend the events we were holding.

The plan was that if anyone of us were talking to a potential candidate, a real talent, we would bring Roy over for an introduction. It was a way of making some of those who came to the reception feel special, and it worked. We had a very successful event that ultimately resulted in the hiring of a number of artists who would move to Los Angeles to work on *Fantasia/2000*.

On a whim, I asked Roy if he had any dinner plans. He lit up some and said, "No!" So I mentioned that I was meeting an old friend for dinner at one of my favorite restaurants in

London called Lemonia and asked if he wanted to join us. He said yes without hesitation. We met in the hotel lobby and grabbed a cab to the restaurant.

Meanwhile, I gave my friend, Christina Schofield, a call and asked her if she would mind if I had a colleague join us for dinner. She was totally fine with it and asked who the person was, to which I responded, "Roy Disney!" There was a pause and then she responded in her lovely British accent, "You're shitting me!"

We arrived at the restaurant and Christina was already there. Lemonia was teeming with patrons, as usual, and we were seated at table next to the open French doors that opened to the sidewalk. It couldn't have been a more perfect evening.

I realized after that evening that anytime I was with Roy, or we were travelling, I would always invite him places. Sometimes he would have another appointment, but often he didn't and would accept the invitation.

On a trip to Walt Disney World, I needed to go over to one of the Disney cruise ships at Port Canaveral. I was working on a stage show for the Disney Cruise Line at the time and wanted to run some animation projection tests in the ship's theater.

I asked Roy if he wanted to go with me and he said sure. Roy loved the cruise ships and enjoyed the trips he'd taken aboard them for special events.

I had several e-mail exchanges with the ship's show producer, to be sure they had the test animation digital files and that everything was working properly, and that there were no technical issues. I mentioned several times that I would be bringing Roy with me, but I didn't think it was having much of an impact. The day before I was coming over to the ship, I sent an e-mail confirming the visit and the tests, and the fact that Roy would be joining me on board the ship.

The show's producer responded to the confirmation and needed Roy's last name so that he could get him the necessary clearance to board the ship while it was in port. When I told him it was Roy Disney, he was stunned. He thought I had been referring to another Roy we both knew.

By the time Roy and I showed up at the ship and walked

The Disney Wonder *at sea*

into the Walt Disney Theater, we were greeted by every executive within a five-mile radius of the *Disney Wonder*. Then, while we were in the theater, the captain of the ship came into the theater to say hello and have a few words with Roy.

Things eventually simmered down, and we were able to run the necessary tests.

All the while, Roy was completely himself—affable and pleasant. He weighed in on the tests we ran and gave some great comments. And had I not asked if he wanted to go, he probably would have been having room service in the hotel and watching television.

Roy was also somewhat shy and would never just invite himself into a situation, but if he felt slighted, he would let you know about it privately. At an official dinner for the Disneyland Paris Park, the planned seating got mixed up. Roy and Patty weren't assigned to the right table.

One of the executives at the time said it all worked out "because Roy's such a generous man and it was fine that Roy was not at the head table; it just was fine."

It was fine until the next day. There was a hand-delivered note to this executive's office. In part it read, "Never forget that I am Roy capital D, capital I, capital S, capital N, capital E, capital Y; D-I-S-N-E-Y, never forget it. Roy." Roy had apparently been really angry about the seating arrangements. According to one executive, "It's the only time I ever saw Roy exercise his Roy Disney card."

On the flip side, one place Roy wasn't shy was when he gave verbal notes in story meetings. Thomas Schumacher, former president of Walt Disney Animation Studios and now president of Disney Theatrical Productions offered up this story:

Work began [on Lilo & Stitch*] and everyone was very excited. The characters, the setting, the attitude, and the story of creating "family" were all landing at each screening.*

And yet, something was wrong with the story. Somewhere deep in the setup of the tale it wasn't working. But of course the rules of this particular game were that the artists creating the film would be in charge. The price tag of this film was a shocking $87 million, which was about half of the cost of the film that came before it.

I asked Roy to sit with me at a screening. He knew how much I loved Chris Sanders and his directing partner, Dean DeBlois. He knew how much it meant

Roy with Thomas Schumacher and Michael Eisner

to me to put this project in their hands and he knew how much was riding on the financial gamble.

After the screening, we went, as was custom, to the recap meeting. These meetings could be brutal and nothing was ever off the table. No one got an easy ride, and this meeting was crucial.

I was the usual host/chair of these meetings and I'd begin each session with sensitivities to various concerns ranging from celebrities in attendance, to financial crises of all proportion, and egos at the edge of disaster.

But with Roy you never had to worry. He was always so honest, always came from love, and always wanted nothing more than a great picture. He never played an angle.

The values of the film were pretty liberal. The film stood for some very modern ideas about the nature of "family" and the voice of the individual.

Roy immediately exclaimed his support for everything on the screen. He loved the theme, he loved the setting, and he loved the characters. BUT, he simply didn't buy Stitch. At that time the character of Stitch was a supercriminal and mastermind of major universal crimes.

Roy just said, "I don't get it. I love watching him. I love being with him. I love how he motivates and enables Lilo, but I just don't buy him."

Chris was silent.

The film was half animated. There was NO turning back.

And Chris listened. Intently.

Roy had no agenda. He had no ax to grind. He just wanted Chris and Dean to make the best movie they could make.

That was the end of the notes. There was nothing else to say. We ended the session. Sometimes these meetings would go on for hours. This one was maybe thirty minutes.

The next day Chris called me and said he had an idea.

Working with existing animation, which could not be changed, Chris turned Stitch into a mutant

Mickey and Roy at the Magic Kingdom,
Walt Disney World, circa 2005

Roy in his office, circa 1986, with *Oliver & Company* storyboards in the background

Roy and Patty during a nature film shoot;
Roy is acting as exterminator as Patty supervises

Patty and Roy, undated

Mickey Mouse with Roy in 1999

Dave Bossert, Joe Grant, and Roy at Joe Grant's ninety-fifth birthday party in the Walt Disney Animation Studios Building in Burbank, California; May 2003

Roy at the Finding Nemo Submarine Voyage
at Disneyland in Anaheim, California, 2008

Patty and Roy

The Roys (left to right): grandson Roy Michael Disney,
son Roy Patrick Disney, and Roy E.

invented by Jumba—who in the original story had
been his partner in crime.

New dialogue was written, cleanup added a lab
coat to Jumba in one scene, sequences that were not
animated we reimagined, and we moved forward.
Suddenly the film made sense. Stitch was a mutant
who had accidentally escaped and needed to be
recovered by his "inventor," Jumba.

It was a marvel of management and artistry.
Everyone believed in the film and worked in sync
to make the changes.

What do we learn from this story? We learn
that a dedicated team can do amazing things when
motivated with clear direction.

We also learn that someone has to say STOP
when things are not right, and to project the
confidence and belief that it can be set right.

That was Roy.

I always think of Roy when I look at Lilo & Stitch.
It was completely reinvented because of him. Stitch
is now all over the company with merchandise,
signage, attractions, parades, and of course the
film, a direct to video sequel, and a TV series.

It became a beautiful film and a force in the
Disney Animation canon because of him.

And for the most part no one knows it.
That's Roy.

Chapter 4
Sailing

One of the things that Roy and I shared an interest in was sailing. I know Roy appreciated that when he told me about his sailing races I actually understood the lingo and understood what he was talking about.

I know my way around a sailboat and once crewed on a boat in a yacht race in the Irish Sea, but Roy was a fierce competitor—he loved to win and had the best equipment, sails, and boats—whatever it took to be the best. I remained a recreational sailor, preferring to putter around sheltered waters in an open day-sailor on a sunny day with a light breeze.

He most loved the thrill of ocean racing, of being on the water with a stiff breeze blowing his boat as fast as she could go.

I was inquisitive about his races and often peppered him

Roy working on Pyewacket

with questions. It was great fun hearing the many stories he had from his years of competitive sailing.

Roy lit up when he talked about the competitiveness of ocean racing, especially when he was racing *Pyewacket* in the Transpac race from Newport Beach, California, to Honolulu, Hawaii. The Transpac is one of the longest ocean races in the world and was first sailed in 1906.

Roy was very competitive and wanted to win the Transpac; he had been chasing a win for years. But in 1997 Roy, recovering from a broken leg, was unable to sail that year in the race. His son Roy Pat took over as skipper and went on to break the race record and win that year. Roy had to greet Roy Pat and the *Pyewacket* crew at the dock in Honolulu

Back: Roy P., Roy E., Rick Brent, Hogan Beatie, Doug Rastello,
Marco Constant, Robbie Haines
Front: Ben Mitchell, Peter Isler, Scott Easom, Dean Barker,
Dick Loewy, Gregg Hedrick

Roy and Patty in Bahrain in the 1960s

Roy and Patty on the sailboat; circa late 1960s

from a wheelchair, but he was so happy that his son had finally won that race.

After that win, Roy decided to have a new *Pyewacket* built at a boatyard in Providence, Rhode Island. Apparently every few years, it was time to employ the latest and greatest in yacht design to have a new, better boat built. As Stanley Gold so aptly put it, "It's an arms race being in that sport!"

Roy built a bigger, faster boat and, in 1999, broke Roy Pat's record and won the Transpac. Nothing like a little family competition!

In 1999, while we were working on *Fantasia/2000*, we flew with Roy to New York to film Itzhak Perlman, the violin virtuoso, for one of the interstitial pieces. Itzhak Perlman is a wonderful person, and we had a great time during the shoot, especially when he did an Elvis impersonation while

Robbie Haines, Roy E., Ben Mitchell

Roy E. at the helm of Pyewacket *with Roy P. as they race to Hawaii in the Transpac*

playing "Blue Suede Shoes" and "Heartbreak Hotel" on his violin.

Once we completed the filming in New York, part of the crew flew to Chicago, and Roy asked if I'd like to stop off in Rhode Island with him to see the progress being made on the new *Pyewacket*. It was only for part of a day, and then we would catch up with the rest of the group in Chicago. Of course I wasn't going to say no to that invitation, and we were off to Providence.

We went to Teterboro Airport in New Jersey to board Roy's plane and take the very short hop up to Providence.

Once we landed we taxied over to the area where the plane would be parked overnight. The crew opened the door and extended the stairway down to the tarmac. I popped down the ladder just as a stretch limousine was pulling around the nose of the aircraft. It was dusk, but you could see through the tinted windows that the pinkish-purple lighting was on inside the passenger compartment.

I turned around to see Roy laughing. He looked down at the copilot, Larry, and said with a broad smile, "Who's that for?"

Larry dutifully responded that it was to take *us* to the hotel. Roy laughed and said that he'd prefer a sedan, which was arranged quite quickly. He instructed the flight crew to take the limo to the hotel, just as a four-door Buick was brought around for us.

We threw our bags into the trunk, and Roy got into the driver's side of the car and drove us to the hotel. We checked in, grabbed a bite to eat, and agreed on a time to meet in the morning for the ride over to the boatyard.

The next morning we drove over to the boatyard where

I was expecting to see a fiberglass boat being built in a shop. Wrong! This was like heading into a top-secret area shrouded in large tarps hiding the boat from prying eyes. This boat was being built with state-of-the-art techniques, and the hull was made out of black carbon fiber, very light-weight and superstrong.

I didn't realize it until that moment how highly secretive this type of yacht racing was, and it truly was an "arms race" of sorts for those who had the money to invest in it. Roy explained that every bit of advantage you could build into the boat made you that much more competitive in a race: it could make the difference between winning and losing. He pointed out that every single item on a boat added weight, and, if you managed that properly, you could have the least

Roy relaxing in a bunk on board Pyewacket

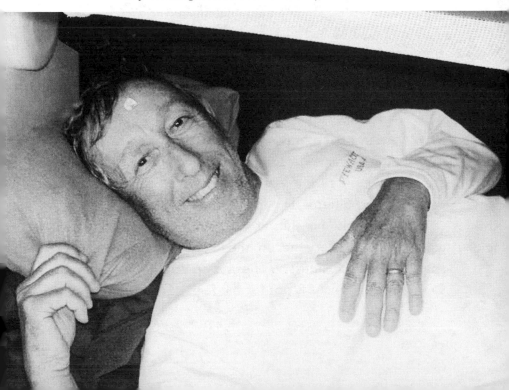

Roy on board Pyewacket

amount of weight possible, thereby making the boat faster through the water. It was one reason why he was having the hull made from carbon fiber.

In retrospect, I think one of the things Roy really loved about ocean racing was that there he could just be one member of a twelve-person sailing crew, one of the guys. It seemed like one of the few places that he could be without being treated differently because of who he was.

He would take his shift at the helm in the middle of the night just like everyone on the crew. Each member had specific responsibilities; no one was on board for a free ride. Sailing in yacht races is not for the faint of heart!

Robbie Haines, project manager for the *Pyewacket*, said:

... when we were in the middle of the Pacific approaching Hawaii, Roy would say, "Man, I would just love to have all my friends around me right now and just show them why I love this sport so much." Because when you're out in the middle of the ocean, you know, all his Disney friends, they don't know what it's like 'cause they're not on board. But the fact that we're out there and the sunsets and the beautiful water, I just remember so many times him saying that. I'd love to have my friends here right now with me so they could witness what I love and realize why I love this sport so much.

The reality was that Roy was down to earth in so many ways, yet he was so very intelligent, well read, and interested in new ways of doing things and new technologies. He truly enjoyed the simplest things that life had to offer, like hot dogs or a really good peanut butter and jelly sandwich.

Robbie Haines in his own words:

Roy loved [the simple things in life]. And he certainly was a simple guy when it came to food. He didn't—I mean I remember on Air Shamrock [Roy's private plane], you know, we didn't have all this

Roy E. and Robbie Haines

Roy and Robbie Haines discussing new sails for Pyewacket

elaborate, fancy meals. He loved hot dogs. He loved peanut butter and jelly.

He would never let me make his peanut butter and jelly sandwiches because he had to have a certain amount of peanut butter on the bread. And he thought that I didn't give him enough. So, you know, when I was in charge of lunch, he'd say Robbie, don't you, don't you make that sandwich, I'll make it!

He loved hot dogs; you know, both he and Patty I think weren't real picky eaters.

And certainly on the boat he wasn't. He loved it when we were going off on long races, like over seven days or so, I remember he'd always get heads of cabbage and he had this concoction he made that tasted so good. After about seven days on a boat

Roy, Leslie, and Robbie Haines

you don't have fresh fruit 'cause it goes bad. But cabbage stays fresh. And he would chop up this cabbage and I think he put mayonnaise in, a little mayonnaise, and then he put in some canned pineapple. And he would just love that, and we'd have it every sixth or seventh or eighth day.

Roy was a real competitor. I mean he loved to win. Somebody once came up to me and asked me why Pyewacket *had such success. And, you know, we always had good equipment. Roy would always want the best boat, sails, everything. But what I think set us apart from our competition was the fact that Roy had this group of guys that were so loyal to him, and he was loyal to us. And we stayed together for fifteen years. I mean that's a big, big part of successful racing. And his competitiveness— we were all equally as competitive—just the combination of him leading us and all of us adoring him so much that I mean we had wonderful success on the water. And it was because of the people, not necessarily the equipment.*

Roy was the type of owner that participated in almost every job on the boat. I mean he cooked, he steered, he would trim the spinnaker, he would grind. You know he would just be a team player. And, that's why we all adored him. I remember a couple of things. I remember the day that I was managing at North Sail Loft in Huntington Beach [California], and I got a call from him. I think he knew who I was, and

Roy E. window at Disneyland Paris

I of course knew who he was. But I'd always wanted to get his business. You know, he had a big seventy-foot sled and he had another sailmaker on his boat. And I wanted, I really wanted, him to get North Sails. So I get this call from Roy out of the blue saying, Robbie, I'd like to come down and meet with you. And being that it's Roy Disney, I said, oh sure Mr. Disney, when would you like to come? And he says, I'd like to come tomorrow or whatever day it was. Well, I have a—I had an office on the second floor of this building and I remember him coming in, in his red Ferrari, smoking a cigarette, which he did at the time. And Roy wasn't one of the more polite smokers. He didn't care where he was, he would have a cigarette in his hand and didn't care what anybody else thought, you know, about his smoking.

He walked into my office and it was a non-smoking office for sure. And he walks in and sits down, and of course being that it's Roy Disney, I scurried around trying to find an ash tray. And he basically sat down and said, "I want to make a change in my sailmaker and I'd like you to help me with it." And that started a wonderful, wonderful relationship.

Roy loved the Transpac race so much; he loved to share stories about the races with his friends and colleagues any chance he could. It was such a big part of his life and something that he was ever passionate about.

He and his second wife, Leslie, had hatched the idea of doing a film called Morning Light *about a diverse group of young adults that would be brought together, trained, and then set out to race in the Transpac.*

Roy went and pitched the idea to the Disney Studios, and the studio agreed to cofund this very cool story about a bunch of kids sailing across the Pacific Ocean to Hawaii.

Robbie Haines went on to say that those in the group, "were from very diverse backgrounds. And one of the best outcomes of that race was this inner city African American kid

Roy and Leslie in front of the Lido Theatre in Newport Beach, California, where the Morning Light *film was playing in release*

Group photo from left to right: Stan Honey, Robbie Haines, Mark Towill, Genny Tulloch, Charlie Enright, Graham Brant-Zawadzki, Jeremy Wilmot, Kate Theisen, Kit Will, Mickey Mouse, Roy, Chris Schubert, Jesse Fielding, Chris Welch, Piet Van Os, Chris Clark, Robbie Kane, Steve Manson, Chris Branning, and Leslie

who saw the notice on the Baltimore [Maryland] Community Sailing Center notice board about the *Morning Light* movie. And he applied. And this one kid, Steve Manson, just wowed everybody."

After the *Morning Light* film was completed and released

The Morning Light *under sail*

Morning Light *premiere at the El Capitan in Hollywood.*
PHOTO BY DOUG GIFFORD

Minnie, Roy, Leslie, and Mickey at the Morning Light *premiere.*
PHOTO BY DOUG GIFFORD

Left to right: Gregg Hedrick, Roy P., and Roy E. are shown in action off Diamond Head (Hawaii's Oahu island), circa 1999.

in the fall of 2008, Roy and Leslie, Robbie and his wife, and Jerry Hauprich helped Steve Manson get into the State University of New York Maritime Academy.

Roy and Leslie took fifteen kids and trained them to become accomplished sailors; many had no sailing background at all, just a desire to learn. Robbie pointed out that "99 percent of them have gone on to bigger and better things in sailing, and Steve Manson's gone on to bigger and better things in education and is gonna end up with a great job when he gets out, all because of the *Morning Light* experience."

Roy at the Morning Light *wrap party*

Chapter 5

Air Roy

Air travel was a real luxury when I was growing up. People would get all dressed up to fly someplace. I didn't even fly until I was sixteen years old.

Nowadays it's not very special to fly on commercial planes. If anything, it has become more of a hassle to travel with cranky flight attendants and service that has slipped even in business class and first class.

But flying in a private plane—well that's a whole other story. So, it is no surprise that there are more stories about Roy's planes than I could possibly fit in this book. Anyone who ever travelled with Roy on his plane has a story to tell, and it usually is something funny or, in some cases, a bit embarrassing. But regardless, there are some wonderful memories for those of us who were lucky enough to fly on Roy's plane—*Air Shamrock*.

Top row (left to right): Roy E., Roy O., and flight attendant. Middle row (left to right): Roy P., Edna, and Patty. Bottom row (left to right): Susan, Abby, and Tim

Air Shamrock *luggage tag, a souvenir of the first flight
I took on Roy's plane!*

Roy actually got his pilot's license when he was sixteen years old, and it was animator Woolie Reitherman, one of Walt's Nine Old Men, who taught him how to fly. He loved to fly and really enjoyed every moment he was in the air. Once, when Roy was newly married to Patty, he went flying in Oregon. He hadn't been flying as often as he had and wasn't paying a lot of attention to his gauges when he realized—the fuel gauge was nearing empty.

That close call, coupled with Patty's concern for him, "took flying his own plane off the list," according to his eldest son, Roy Patrick.

But he did love flying in his private plane, and he loved to spoil those who flew with him. He always wanted people to sit in the jump seat in the cockpit during takeoff or landing. It gave him great pleasure to watch people enjoy the experience.

I had the pleasure of sitting in the cockpit of the *Challenger* (the smaller jet Roy had before getting his Boeing 737) for landings in London; Dublin; Oakland, California; Orlando, Florida; and Providence, Rhode Island. It was just an opportunity that you have to grab when it is offered; it brings a whole new perspective to flying.

Flying into Honolulu in the jump seat of the Challenger.
PHOTO BY LESLIE DEMEUSE DISNEY

March 1995 trip aboard Roy E.'s private jet to Pixar included the following participants: front row (left to right): Roy, Don Ernst, and David Lovegren; middle row (left to right): Scott Johnson, Dave Bossert (book's author), and Steve Goldberg; back row (left to right): Neil Eskurie, Ed Kummer, and Hendel Butoy

One of the fun things about flying with Roy on the *Challenger* was that wherever you went, the flight crew would order food for the flights from restaurants near the airports. On one trip, we had to make a refueling stop in Burlington, Vermont. Some really tasty treats were delivered right to the plane.

On our return trip, while we were still over the north Atlantic, the flight crew called ahead to order a variety of Italian food. Roy would ask everyone on the plane what they were in the mood for—generally majority ruled.

We had to clear passport control and customs. When

we landed at Burlington Airport the plane taxied over to a small building. The customs agent came out, walked across the tarmac, and boarded the plane. He obviously knew Roy, based on his greeting, and he proceeded to collect our passports and went back to his office to do the clearances.

Meanwhile the Italian food, including some pizza, was delivered, and the flight attendant was taking care of all that while we waited for the passports to be returned. Once we were back in the air and at our cruising altitude, it was time for dinner. The flight attendant quickly got the food unpacked and readied. She took our orders and it was about as pleasant a meal as I've ever had.

Just when we thought it couldn't get any better, out came ice cream sundaes as we were flying over the Continental Divide. When we arrived at Burbank Airport and the plane had taxied over to the *Shamrock* hangar, there was still one more surprise. None of us were aware of it at the time, but the flight attendant had been picking up various treats from the different European cities we stopped in. She had assembled a small basket of chocolates, cookies, and other goodies for each of us: parting gifts to bring home!

As I said, travelling with Roy could make for one very spoiled person.

When *Air Shamrock* upgraded to the 737, things got even better. There was more room to wander about and stretch your legs. The plane could fly nonstop from the Van Nuys Airport in Los Angeles to Europe.

On the smaller *Challenger*, you would typically have a meal at the seat you were in. But on the 737, there was actually a dining room. It was nice to leave your seat and eat as group; it was very elegant.

Roy relaxing on board his plane

The extra room would come in handy for a special passenger on a return trip from Walt Disney World to Burbank. Roy's oldest son, Roy Pat, had come on the trip, and, while we were doing some business, Roy Pat went off on his own. Unbeknownst to us, he had gone off to Walt

Disney World's landscape nursery to pick up a birthday gift for his neighbor, actor Andy Garcia.

Andy and his wife are big Disney fans. So, Roy Pat had stopped by the nursery to pick up a Mickey Mouse topiary; it would prove to be a very unique gift and not one that you could go pick up at the local home center.

Roy Pat figured it would fit in the cargo hold of his father's 737 to be transported back to Burbank. But he had miscalculated: the topiary was too tall to fit in through the cargo hold hatch without it potentially being damaged.

The next thing we knew, the Mickey topiary was being brought in through the passenger door and stored in the forward galley of the plane for the trip back. Roy E. seemed a little displeased but didn't say anything. Roy was not going to make an issue out of it, especially with guests on the plane.

Needless to say the topiary made it back to Burbank in one piece and was a big hit as a birthday gift.

Sometimes when you flew with Roy, there would be a side trip or some sort of unexpected adventure. It seemed like everybody who flew with Roy a few times would have some story to tell about an unscheduled side trip.

Thomas Schumacher in his own words:

Everyone who loved Roy Disney probably has a thousand stories. There are stories about his love of the Animation Department. Stories of his years as an inveterate smoker (Roy didn't just smoke—he made it a signature), and of course the stories of travel on "Air Roy."

In my case they all blend together, but here is a favorite.

Travelling with Roy (and Patty) was an honor and a treat not to be missed. Within my circle we referred to travel in three categories: commercial, a Disney jet (owned by the company), and Air Roy— the personal Disney Family plane. Yes, before 1995 (the year of the great cessation), you did have to accept the fact that the plane would carry a certain "Turkish Market" quality of air with both of them puffing away, but it was still magical to be with them.

When the plane took off they would hold hands. Each liftoff was so dear as they took their places and formed that bond. Sometimes passengers would react in mild terror that their flying hosts were praying, but Roy and Patty just laughed it off. This was a ritual not to be missed.

On one particular trip, we were putting together the music elements of Fantasia/2000. One of the great honors of that project is that the renowned conductor James Levine was overseeing our music. That particular summer "Jimmy," as everyone working with him calls him, was conducting in Vienna and our only way to meet was to hop on "Air Roy" and head off.

Our travelling party included animation directors Hendel Butoy and Leon Joosen, who were, like anyone else would be, mesmerized by

*crossing the globe on a private aircraft. Roy was
always generous that way. He didn't suggest others
should "meet him there." He loved filling the plane
with artists and sharing his time, his sailing
videos, his stories, and his unabashed love for life
with them.*

*All things in Vienna went swimmingly, and we
were advised that on the way back to the States,
we'd be stopping in Spain to drop Roy and a bunch
of cargo off so that he could commence the Route
of Columbus race across the Atlantic. The race
literally follows the route of the* Nina, *the* Pinta,
and the Santa Maria. *Roy, his crew, and his beloved
sailboat* Pyewacket *were all to meet up with our
plane.*

*Given that we were dropping him off on a Friday
afternoon, I asked if we might hang with him for the
weekend in Spain before heading back. Roy beamed.
He didn't want to waste our time, so he assumed
we'd want to head immediately back to California.
Hardly!!*

*We arrived via Air Roy in Cadiz, Spain. I'd been
in charge of arranging for car services to pick us
up and drive us around Austria, but Roy said he'd
handle the "cars" in Spain.*

*As we landed, the customary limos were not on
the tarmac. I thought I'd made some terrible error
and again said to Roy, "You were doing the cars,
right?" He confirmed yes, and when I probed about*

where they were, he said, "At the Hertz counter!" Oh. We were going on a motoring trip.

Dutifully we went inside and arranged a small sedan and a station wagon to transport the gear he'd brought for the sailing crew. Unfortunately they didn't have maps of any kind. Roy pointed out that it couldn't be that hard. Just head south for an hour and then head for the water. Oh. Again.

We hopped in our cars with no addresses in our pockets. Or cell phones. With Roy in the lead, and Hendel, Leon, and I in tow.

We pulled out of the gate, and all I saw was a blur. Roy was notorious for driving fast, but given the circumstances, I foolishly thought we'd drive in tandem searching for "the sails" and a harbor.

Hendel hung out the window shouting, "I think I see him" and I did my best Formula One impersonation as we raced through villages and on highways. At one point I swear we ended up on a dirt road with chickens squawking and dashing out of our way, while the car antenna picked up laundry drying on lines between houses.

After many stops, many circles, and many hand gestures with locals, we did in fact find the harbor. Roy screeched to a halt, jumped out of the car, pointed to his boat in the distance, and off we raced to the finish line, laughing with him all the way.

*Just getting there was a great victory. And that
was Roy. He found joy and delights around every
corner.*

The adventures were sometimes on board the plane as
well. This was especially true for the first-timers on Air Roy. It
was always enjoyable to travel with someone who had never
been on a private plane before.

Wendy Lefkon in her own words:

*Getting to know Roy has been one of the great
joys of my career at Disney. In 1997, I worked closely
with him on a biography of his dad being written by
Bob Thomas. We went through several drafts, and
once the book was edited and printed we decided to
send Roy on a tour to help publicize the book. When
he called to ask me to join him on the tour I was,
needless to say, very excited.*

*We did a wonderful event at the Disney Store in
New York City, and the next day we would fly off to
Chicago.*

*We left from Teterboro Airport, in New Jersey, and,
about forty-five minutes into the flight, I needed to
use the restroom. I opened the door to a cavernous
space that had lots of things in it—but for the life
of me I could not actually find the thing I needed
most—the toilet. I was opening doors to closets and
other storage areas all the while trying to decide*

how much longer I should wait before going back into the cabin and asking for help. Luckily just then I saw an upholstered bench that I realized could be lifted. And there it was! The toilet. Both I and my bladder were quite relieved—literally.

And then I told everyone what had happened. And I realized that wanting to share that story, which was a little embarrassing, said a lot about Roy. He was so welcoming and so easy to be with that it seemed natural to share my moment in the john.

We landed in Chicago—with me in the cockpit jump seat—and as I was going to deplane he insisted I pause at the top of the stairs to the tarmac and do a "royal wave."

We travelled around the country for a week, and I'll never forget one minute of the special time we spent together.

Probably one of the most poignant things many of us had seen over the years is how Roy and Patty would hold hands during takeoffs and landings. It was a very simple thing but a powerful image that had an impact on many, including John Lasseter and his wife, Nancy.

John Lasseter in his own words:

I was flying with him on his plane; [it's] one of my fondest memories because we were inspired by

Left to right: David Jessen, Les Perkins, Dave Bossert, Stan Deneroff, Roy E. Disney, Roy P. Disney, Shawn Anderson, and Tye Arnold; photo taken at Orlando International Airport in Florida at the end of the True-Life Adventures DVD film shoot

Roy and Patty. We were so touched that every time they took off in their plane they held hands. No matter where they were in the plane. She may have been sitting behind him and he would hold his hands up over him. But they'd reach across the aisle and they would hold hands. And I saw that numerous times. And Nancy and I do that to this day, inspired by them.

Left to right: David Jessen, Les Perkins, Dave Bossert, Stan Deneroff, Roy E. Disney, and Roy P. Refueling in Burlington, Vermont, as we returned from a trip abroad to London and Dublin

Chapter 6
The Company

On a trip to Orlando in 2005, Roy and I went to Downtown Disney for dinner one evening before seeing the Cirque du Soleil show "La Nouba." Downtown Disney is an open-air shopping district that has a nice mix of restaurants, shops, and entertainment venues.

We decided to have dinner that evening in the upstairs dining room of Wolfgang Puck's restaurant. The ground floor was more café style, and the upstairs a bit more quiet.

Being with Roy at one of the parks was always interesting because invariably he would be recognized. Most people were respectful, but there were always some fans that would approach him even if he was in the middle of eating. It was no surprise that a few heads turned as we were seated at a table in the restaurant.

Toward the end of our meal, I noticed a family of three

Mickey and Roy at Magic Kingdom Walt Disney World, circa 2005

seated several tables away looking at us. The little girl, who was maybe seven or eight years old, got up from her table and started walking, rather shyly, toward our table. You could tell that she had worked up a lot of courage to come over to our table by herself; she was smiling nervously and looked back at her parents a few times for reassurance that what she was doing was okay.

As she came to a stop at the edge of our table, Roy looked at her with a big smile and then said, "Hello!" She looked back and forth at us both momentarily and then looked at Roy and said, "Mr. Disney."

Roy responded, "Yes!"

The little girl continued: "I wanted to thank you for building a really great park. Me and my family have really had a good time here."

Roy responded, still beaming with a smile, and said, "Why

thank you very much. Are you and your family enjoying your visit?"

The little girl responded, "Oh, yes; we have gone on a lot of rides and it's been very, very fun."

Roy looked at her with a broad smile and said, "Well, I'm glad to hear that. You tell your mom and dad that I'm glad they took you here to the park."

She responded, "I will!"

The little girl quickly skipped back to her parents. They smiled and gave a wave of thanks. It was one of those moments that they will cherish for a lifetime: a story that they will relay to family and friends of the evening that their daughter met Roy Disney at Disney World!

It was a moment that to me summed up what it is like to work at The Walt Disney Company. Those moments come along from time to time when you least expect it, but they

Goofy, Donald, Mickey, Minnie, and Pluto: the fab five at Disney World in Orlando, Florida

Mickey and Roy, Disneyland, Anaheim, 2008

are a reminder that what we do at this great family entertainment company has such a profound and moving impact on so many people. It is what each of us company "cast members" does daily in our various disciplines that touches the very heart and soul of our "guests" the world over.

Roy knew that; he knew that it was all about quality entertainment and value to a legion of loyal fans. He knew what his name and the company meant to so many, and everything he did at the studio was centered on that one simple principle—quality. Roy said:

> One of the things that Walt understood was that art is great, but it is the artists who make it that are who you have to believe in; who you have to put your trust in and your faith in. I wanted the studio to continue to think of itself as a group of artists and not a commercial enterprise only. . . . It's one of the things that I'm proudest of. The thing that drove Walt certainly drives me too, and drives most artists, is keeping balls in the air and making stuff better all the time. You don't do stuff by yourself in this business; you got to say "we" all the time in this business.

Peter Schneider, the former president of Disney Animation and former chairman of the Walt Disney Studios, said that Roy once conveyed a little story about a gardener that illustrated how you underestimated Roy at your own peril. It was in the context of being asked why he was so laid back about some unpleasant things that were going on at the company. Roy said about being laid back:

> I'm like that guy in the garden with the hoe. I'm sitting in my chair and a snake comes out of the hole and goes around and I just sit there in my chair watching what the snake is doing, not caring, looking the other way. And after awhile, the snake's not paying attention to me and I'm looking away but have my fingers on my hoe and then whap; the snake's dead!

Roy, in Legends Plaza with the Team Disney Building in the background

Roy resigned from the Disney Board of Directors in 1983 during a takeover battle with a financier who was looking to carve up the company and sell off the pieces. Financier Saul P. Steinberg thought the company, if it were sold off in pieces separately, would be worth more than the company as a whole. He wanted to sell off the theme parks, the film library, and other assets.

Steinberg was also engaging in what was known at the time as "greenmail," in which a company buys a block of its own stock back from a specific person, in this case Steinberg, as opposed to making the purchase on the stock exchange. This strategy involves the company paying a premium price, higher than what it might cost in the open market, for the stock—hence the obvious correlation to blackmail.

As *Forbes* magazine noted, ". . . he did force Disney to pay him an almost $60 million premium for his shares, which helped put the word *greenmail* into the financial lexicon." This was after Steinberg had amassed an 11 percent stake in the company, and Roy had resigned his board seat. Then CEO Ron Miller justified it by saying Steinberg was "motivated by greed" and that he didn't want him "to come back and rape the company again."

Miller and his management team had recruited some "white knights" to come in and buy up a large stake in the company. Sid Bass, his brothers, and father became the largest shareholders in The Walt Disney Company in 1984, which

Disney Board meeting, with Roy O. (center), Disney's chairman at the time; Roy E. (front left); Cardon Walker (to the left of Roy E.); and Ron Miller (directly across from Roy E.), Walt's son-in-law; and others attending, circa 1969

helped to stave off Steinberg or anyone else who was thinking of coming after the company.

They also asked Roy to come back on the Board of Directors to help show solidarity. Roy agreed, provided that they gave him three board seats: for Roy, his business partner, Stanley Gold, and his brother-in-law Peter Daily.

Once Roy was back on the board, it was clear that the company needed a new management team, and, with allies

This is a photo of a signed memento given to Roy from the artists in the Animation Department when Roy returned to the company after the successful conclusion of the "Greenmail" takeover attempt. This hung in Roy's office until his death.

on the board, they were able to co-opt the Bass brothers to help make that change. With the support of the largest shareholders, they were able to recruit Frank Wells and Michael Eisner as that new management team.

According to Roy, it was Frank Wells—an old classmate from Pomona College—who he hoped would be the new CEO of the company. But as Stanley Gold recalls, Frank actually wanted to be co-CEO with Michael Eisner. However, Eisner refused that notion and would not agree to come on board unless he was made the CEO. Frank graciously acquiesced and was fine with becoming president of the company.

Walt Disney was quoted as saying, "I have no use for people who throw their weight around as celebrities, or for those who fawn over you just because you are famous." That incident with Michael wanting to be CEO may have been, in hindsight, a telltale sign of things to come.

Roy once told me that it all boiled down to him sitting in the living room of his Toluca Lake home as to whether to take the company private or not. He had lined up support to the tune of $2 billion and had the management team to step in and turn the company around. In the end he opted to keep the company a public entity and put the new management team in place to run it.

This created a deep rift between Roy and his cousin Diane Disney Miller, daughter of Walt Disney and wife of then CEO Ron Miller, who was forced out of the company. They didn't speak for many years after that, and it was only in the last ten years or so of his life that he actually had some contact via notes and the occasional phone call with Diane. He told me once that while on the phone with Diane he heard Ron screaming in the background because he knew she was on the phone with Roy; some wounds never heal.

In reflecting on the management change out in 1984, Stanley Gold pointed out that those in charge at the time were "pretty afraid at that point anyways." He went on to say that "the decision in 1984 to change management and find people who had talent to resurrect the studio was Roy's. I will take credit for engineering it—the tactical, how to do it, who to get allied with, but the real decision on doing it—and it was at huge risk to him—was Roy's."

Stanley explained:

We had a sort of a rally call. Actually coined by Patty at the time, and it was "all the way in or all the way out." Meaning, you couldn't stay on the outside and just complain that they're (current management) making bad movies and making bad decisions. You needed to either get all the way in and try to change it, or get all the way out: meaning that the other option was to sell the stock, move on! We already had Shamrock and were doing okay. And diversify into non-Disney stuff. And that was an option I gave Roy in Christmas 1983. And he said, no, I'm not walking away from the studio. Let's go fight for it.

Roy believed in the "mission of The Walt Disney Company." It transcended everything because it was his family's legacy and that was something that was more than worth fighting for. Roy and Patty were "all the way in," and, for them, there was no other choice.

*Roy at the Disney Animation exhibit at the
Disney California Adventure Park*

Regardless of the family rift, Roy's decision resulted in the awakening of a sleeping giant; with the new management team of Eisner and Wells in place, the company began a period of explosive growth. Roy became the vice chairman of The Walt Disney Company and chairman of the Animation Department overseeing what in hindsight is now referred to as the "renaissance" of animation or the "Second Golden Age of Disney Animation."

According to Stanley Gold:

> *He just wanted to get back in there and make it right. He had the option to walk away. He had enough money to sell his shares and live like a gentleman for the rest of his life. He just couldn't do it. It was his heritage. This was his birthright, and he was going to give it an effort to fix it or die trying. Or more likely go broke trying.*

Eisner and Wells

Gold noted, "The first ten years were phenomenal." He said:

You had two guys who were back in Hollywood. Michael knew how to make movies fabulous. Knew the elements, knew character, knew script, and knew actors, actresses; knew music. And Frank knew how to put the pieces together. They were back, and then they brought in twenty-five guys who were all pretty experienced. I mean what Disney didn't have is any of the population from any of the other studios. For some internal reason, old management thought that was a bad thing to do.

Essentially, Michael Eisner and Frank Wells went hunting for great talent that could make great movies for the studio.

Meanwhile, Roy presided over a succession of hits, including *The Little Mermaid*, *Beauty and the Beast*, *Aladdin*, *The Lion King*, and *Pocahontas*.

After the phenomenal success of *The Little Mermaid*, Jeffrey Katzenberg became a convert to animation. He saw the potential of this art form and focused much more attention on the animation division. Jeffrey became a big fan and supporter of the artists, rewarding the animation team with bonuses for the success of *The Little Mermaid*: a first for the group in many years at that point.

Beauty and the Beast became the first animated feature film to be nominated for Best Picture at the Academy Awards alongside four-live action films. On January 30, 1992, it also became the first animated film to break $100 million at the

WALT DISNEY PICTURES
PRESENTS

THE

LION KING

The

most

beautiful

love

story

ever

told.

WALT DISNEY PICTURES

presents

Beauty and the Beast

domestic box office. Just a few years later, on June 15, 1994, *The Lion King* would explode at the box office, going on to amass a then staggering $312,855,561 domestic gross in its initial release.

Roy also ushered in and supported the wide use of computer technology in the animation process with the creation of the Computer Animation Production System, also known as CAPS.

The Walt Disney Animation Studios team that developed CAPS is honored with a Technical Achievement Award at the Motion Picture Academy of Arts & Scienes Scientific & Technical Awards in 1992. Left to right: Mark Kimball, Peter Nye, Michael Shantzis, David Wolf, Peter Schneider (president of Walt Disney Animation, speaking at the podium), Tom Hahn, Randy Cartwright, Lem Davis, Dave Coons, Jim Houston; Dylan Kohler was added to the award at a later date and was not present at the banquet.

CAPS, another technological leap forward for Disney Animation, used computers and and custom software to do digital ink and paint as well as compositing of the animation. The system used computers that were made by a then small hardware company that was manufacturing high-end graphics computers known as the Pixar Image Computer.

Roy saw the value in new technology, which has been a hallmark of the company since his uncle and father started the studio. The studio had the first cartoon with synchronized sound with *Steamboat Willie*; the first color cartoon with *Flowers and Trees*; the first animated feature film with *Snow White and the Seven Dwarfs*; and a litany of other firsts.

But he needed to get funding to implement the CAPS system into the Animation Department. He knew there was value in automating and making the hand-drawn animation process more efficient, both from a scheduling and budget standpoint, but also because this was the next natural step in the development of the animation process.

Michael Eisner, Frank Wells, and Jeffery Katzenberg, then chairman of the Disney Studios, initially didn't want to invest in the computer hardware because they believed that Disney was in the business of making products and films. At the time they didn't fully believe that the Animation division was all that viable, having just come to the company on the heels of *The Black Cauldron*: a costly flop.

In fact, when this new management team came to the company, they wanted to shut down animation—they didn't understand it, and it had lost money in recent years. Fortunately, Roy placed himself in the position of essentially being the godfather of the Animation division.

Peter Schneider remembers:

Roy wanted to up the artist quality of the animation movies and knew in his heart the key was to get the CAPS system built, but Frank, Michael, and Jeffrey said we don't invest in hardware. We're a software company, we make products, and we don't make machines. But Roy was dog-it and stuck to his guns and pushed Frank. One day with a smile he said to me, "Well I got it done" and he never explained how. He just was Roy and got things done. And without the CAPS system, we would never have done a damn thing. We would never have revolutionized the animation business, and Pixar would never have happened without the CAPS system.

Peter Schneider, Roy Disney, and Jeffrey Katzenberg

John Lasseter in his own words:

When we were formulating our new company, Pixar, Steve Jobs brought us in February of 1986 from Lucas Film. The very first contract, the very first income, which Pixar received, was the deal with Disney Animation and Roy Disney to create the CAPS system. It was a joint venture with Disney. And we were providing all the technology, and they were providing the know-how, as far as how they wanted it laid out. It revolutionized Disney Animation with the last scene in The Little Mermaid *to* The Rescuers Down Under *onward.*

So, it was Roy, and it's that support, you know, of doing it right. And so when Disney Animation turned around with The Little Mermaid, *and it became this second kind of . . . second Golden Age of Disney Animation, you know, it's all because of him.*

In essence, when Roy believed in something, he found a way to make it happen. With Frank Wells, Michael Eisner, and Jeffrey Katzenberg just coming into the company, none of them had any understanding of animation or the animation process, and it was an area, at that time, that was not generating much revenue for the company compared to the annual overhead cost of the Animation Department. Roy got what he needed to improve the

Roy with Jeffrey Katzenberg during production on
Beauty and the Beast; early 1991

Animation Department because they were trying to keep him happy.

According to Schneider, CAPS and *Fantasia/2000* are two of the biggest examples of things that Roy just said "we're doing this." But he also pointed out that Roy saw a need for other improvements around the company and acted on his instincts, where others didn't quite get it initially.

Peter Schneider in his own words:

I'll give you another one that Roy was solely instrumental for, the Character Voice Department.

Peter Schneider and Roy Disney
PHOTO BY LESLIE DISNEY

Okay, now that was a luncheon that Roy and I had where he had just come back from Argentina, and Mickey Mouse's voice didn't sound like Mickey Mouse's voice. And we had lunch, and I said well the only way to do this, to get consistency with the character voices, Roy, is to start your own department. And we crafted the whole thing over lunch, and he then championed it and pushed it through the company. I know that Michael and Jeffrey were not happy with the costs and resisted, but, in the end, the artist results that Roy wanted not only made the movies better but also created more revenue for the company because of the quality.

It made all the movies we've made better because they were dubbed correctly; it standardized Mickey Mouse and Donald, all the characters. But where the real revenue came from was having in place Von Johnson and Jeff Miller, who were able to take the English language movies and make them beautiful.

So that when we made Little Mermaid, *it was translated correctly into all the languages, which in turn generated money. So, yes, so we spent a million dollars in the Character Voice Department, but the return was much greater. And Roy just bullheaded it through. CAPS,* Fantasia/2000, *and lots more. And Roy was dismissed by both Michael and Jeffrey as having no value—that's the sad thing.*

There was a slow and steady deterioration in the relationship between Eisner and Katzenberg that accelerated after the death of Frank Wells in early 1994. Wells, who was president of The Walt Disney Company, was an avid mountain climber and adventurer who set out with Richard Bass to climb the seven highest peaks on the seven continents. They were able to reach the top of six: Kilimanjaro in Africa, Kosciuszko in Australia, Elbrus in Europe, Vinson in Antarctica, McKinley in North America, and Aconcagua in South America; but Everest eluded them after two failed attempts.

Then Frank was killed in a helicopter crash during a backcountry skiing trip in Nevada. It was a shocking tragedy that happened on Easter Sunday 1994. In hindsight, it was this accident that was the beginning of the end for that stellar growth period from the previous decade through the mid-1990s.

For ten years Eisner and Wells worked together in reviving the Disney Company, and took it from Roy's living room in 1984 when it was valued at between $2 and $3 billion dollars to more than $22 billion by 1994. It was all due to Roy, all of which he engineered after he resigned from the Disney Board of Directors and made the decision to recruit Eisner and Wells in order to turn the company around.

But once Frank Wells was gone, Roy's relationship with Eisner started to sour. Stanley Gold recalled, "It wasn't so obvious at the beginning. [Frank Wells's] death occurred Easter Sunday 1994. I don't think, at least, to me, and I probably was more keenly aware of this than anyone, it wasn't so evident to me that things were beginning to run amok until we got into 1996, 1997."

Shortly after Wells died, Jeffrey Katzenberg lobbied for the position of company president. That was not to be. Katzenberg left the company in September of 1994.

After Katzenberg's departure from Disney, he partnered with Steven Spielberg and David Geffen to form DreamWorks SKG, which had live-action and animation units, with Jeffrey at the helm of animation.

Not long after DreamWorks Animation was established, there was much more competition for animators industrywide. Jeffrey made attractive offers to artists across a variety of disciplines and was known to call people at home; he could be quite persuasive.

Toward the end of the 1990s, Roy's relationship with Michael Eisner was deteriorating rapidly and the two were estranged. Ultimately board member John Bryson, who was the chairman of the Governance and Nominating Committee, delivered the news to Roy at a restaurant in Pasadena that he would not be renominated to the Board of Directors. Roy was furious when he recounted the story. In spite of his removal from the board, Disney still had some fight left in him. It was his family's company, and as in 1984, he would go all in to fight for it.

Roy resigned before the board vote. He ended his resignation letter stating:

In conclusion, Michael, it is my sincere belief that it is you who should be leaving and not me. Accordingly, I once again call for your resignation or retirement. The Walt Disney Company deserves fresh, energetic leadership at this challenging time in its history, just as it did in 1984 when I headed a restructuring which resulted in your recruitment to the Company.

I have, and will always have, an enormous allegiance and respect for this Company, founded by my uncle, Walt, and father, Roy, and to our faithful employees and loyal stockholders. I don't know if you and other directors can comprehend how painful it is for me and the extended Disney family to arrive at this decision.

Patty and Roy Disney with Ilene and Stanley Gold on a trip to Antarctica

Within a few weeks Roy and his business partner, Stanley Gold, launched the SaveDisney.com Web site, which allowed them to take their fight directly to the fans and shareholders.

In March of 2004, Roy and Stanley hosted their own shareholders' meeting the day before the actual company shareholders meeting in Philadelphia. Stanley Gold recalled that the day before, "We wrote to all the shareholders on SaveDisney.com. 'We've rented the hotel ballroom across the street from the conference center. At three o'clock, Roy will address them, Stanley will say a few words, and we'll give you our ideas as to why we oppose this management." The line to get into the meeting with Roy and Stanley stretched around the block.

Left to right: Dave Smith, Mike Vaughn, Richard Sherman, Roy E. Disney, and Howard Green

Son Tim Disney with his children and father

Roy, with his dog Lucy

Roy at a *Fantasia/2000* event in early 2000

Roy E., sitting with the bronze statue of his father,
Roy O., and Minnie Mouse, in the Legends Plaza at the
Walt Disney Studios, Burbank, California

Roy with his daughter Abigail

Laurie Gilbert, Leslie, and Roy E. Disney in Hawaii

Roy and Robbie Haines getting into an eighty-degree heated pool in Hawaii after Leslie insisted they needed a workout. PHOTO BY LESLIE DEMEUSE DISNEY

Roy and Leslie enjoy a Hawaiian sunset.

Roy and Mickey at the Walt Disney World Magic
Kingdom, Orlando, Florida, 2005

**Stanley Gold, in his own words,
further recounting the gathering:**

*Roy went outside, and I realized how beloved he
was. People would kiss him. Women wanted him
to write Roy Disney across their T-shirts, sign their
Mickey Mouse ears. And in fact, at four o'clock—an
hour past the time we were supposed to begin—we
found him out in the street with the people, still in
his deck shoes, not in his coat and tie. He was the
true icon of the company. You could see it on the
streets of Philadelphia.*

Michael Eisner eventually left the company earlier than
he had planned. Stanley Gold recalls, "Roy said, 'I think the
company's gone through enough turmoil, let's see if we can
patch it up.' So, I called Bob [Iger], and we had breakfast at
Roy's house." Roy returned to the company.

Sadly, the battle had taken a toll on Roy. The spark that he
had for animation when I first met him had been diminished.
It wasn't extinguished (I don't think that was ever possible),
but it was much less evident. He was still the ever-present
cheerleader for Disney Animation, but he didn't have the
drive he once did, he didn't have the desire to pilot another
big project. Don Hahn and I met with Roy a few times in
2007 and 2008 to talk about another "Fantasia" movie—but
it was not to be.

Roy had made peace with Bob Iger. According to Stanley
Gold, "Roy thought Bob can eat in a hamburger line or he

Roy Disney receiving his Disney Legends award in 1998 with actress Hayley Mills on the left and Glynis Johns on the right

Thirty-fifth anniversary of Disneyland brought out the stars, including (left to right): Minnie Mouse, Roy E., Michael Eisner, Ronald Reagan, Art Linkletter, Bob Cummings, Mickey Mouse, and Frank Wells.

can eat fancy. But he's a people person, and I think Roy liked that. Roy was that kind of a guy."

In conversation, Roy told me he had great respect for Bob Iger and was particularly pleased that Bob had first established a great relationship with Steve Jobs and Pixar and then acquired the company.

A still-frame of the two Fate Heads from the Disney Academy Award-nominated Destino, *in 2003*

Chapter 7
Destino *and the Academy Awards*

The short film *Destino* had a very, very long path to completion. It was a project that was not planned for but rather grew out of a chance meeting in 1946 between Salvador Dali and Walt Disney. Legend has it that Walt and Dali had met at a party hosted by Jack Warner of Warner Bros. fame. The two artists immediately hit it off.

They had admired one another and agreed to work together on a project, which ultimately turned out to be *Destino*.

Dali actually worked at the Disney Studios in Burbank for about eight months. Walt had paired him with a legendary Disney artist named John Hench, who had the uncanny ability to mimic Dali's style but also to bring it into the realm of animation.

The short film was planned as a segment for a packaged film but was never completed. A packaged film was really a collection of shorts strung together into a feature, like a *Fantasia*, *Melody Time*, or *Make Mine Music*.

The *Destino* short was not completed in 1946 for various reasons, most notably the financial pressure that the studio was experiencing after the end of World War II. That coupled with the fact that the short had such a Dali-centric stylistic influence that was visually at odds with the Disney house style and possibly viewed as overshadowing Walt Disney and the Disney brand.

The Dali artwork would lay dormant in the company archives for the next forty years or so. According to Ed Nowak, deputy general counsel for The Walt Disney Company, "The first time I think I can remember it coming up with Roy was as a result of Frank Wells's interest in the fact that the new management in the late 1980s had realized the studio had a treasure trove of Dali art for *Destino*."

Ed explained that senior management wanted a valuation of the artwork to understand what the company had as an asset; Nowak said, ". . . and then no one talked about it again for years. There were these initial conversations, and then one day I get a call from Roy, which was a real event because I'm not sure I had ever really talked to him before or talked to him at any length about anything before." Roy said to Ed, "I'd like to make that movie."

In late 1998 the artwork that was created for *Destino* resurfaced while we were working on *Fantasia/2000*.

Roy suggested that we put some of the *Destino* art into an interstitial. Many of us had heard about the Dali artwork but had never actually seen it. We had eventually brought all of the Dali and Hench artwork that they created for *Destino* out of storage and did high-resolution digital scans of each of the roughly 150 pieces of art.

Though the art didn't make it into *Fantasia/2000*, we did turn it into a short film, which was completed in 2003. All of us, including Roy, felt that it was a great honor to work on a project that was started over a half century earlier by two of the most venerable artists of the twentieth century.

Ed Nowak in his own words:

Roy had one of the qualities that I really came to love about dealing with him: that was once you got involved in something with him, no matter who you were or what discipline you were coming from, he kept you involved.

And so as this thing unfolded, he would say, wow, I'm going to have it made and I want you to come over. We're going to look at the Dali drawings. We're going to look at the Hench drawings. I want you to talk to John Hench. Let's figure out what's Dali and what's Hench. Let's try to assemble what the story was and we've got to put that back together again. And, so I find myself, in a room with Roy and John Hench and a couple of other people, as though my input were really of any value to them. But, he knew that I was kind of an enthusiast and wanted to help.

*As a layman in this area, we would talk about
things like, are we going to use the old recording;
are we going to rerecord; if you do, can we edit?
There were all kinds of little other questions that
came up. He could have had other people doing it.
But because, you know, a rapport on this thing had
developed, he just kept coming back to me, and I
was delighted. And he kept me involved with this
right up through the completion.*

*Then when it was done, somewhere between
when it was done and the exhibition in Spain, word
got back to me that there had been a meeting with
the troops, where the original artwork was all
pulled out and it was available for us, the internal
people, to look at. And Roy got up and gave a speech
to the people involved with the picture, and Roy said
that me, Ed Nowak, was responsible for* Destino.
And I said, "What?"

When Roy told the story, he basically said that if it weren't
for Ed Nowak, *Destino* might never have been made. Ed
was the one guy at the studio who doggedly went through
all of the associated paperwork and cleared up any internal
matters that might have been a stumbling block to completing the movie.

It was even more thrilling when the film started to win
awards. In 2003 *Destino* won Best Animated Short at the
Rhode Island International Film Festival, the Jury Award of
Merit at the Palm Springs International ShortFest, the Grand

Prix at the Melbourne International Film Festival in Australia, and a Certificate of Merit at the Chicago International Film Festival.

In early 2004 *Destino* won a Special Citation at the Los Angeles Film Critics Association Awards. This was followed by a nomination for an Annie Award, which is an animation award given out annually by The International Animated Film Society, ASIFA-Hollywood. And then the ultimate nod came when *Destino* was nominated for an Oscar by the Academy of Motion Picture Arts and Sciences.

Those of us who worked on the film were overjoyed; Roy, who was executive producer, and Dominique Monfray, the director, were the two nominees. Roy was immensely proud of the fact that not only did we complete the film started by his Uncle Walt, but that it had been nominated for the most prestigious film award in the world!

As the date approached for the Seventy-sixth Academy Awards show, February 29, 2004, arrangements were made for Roy and Patty; one of the film's producers, Baker Bloodworth; Dominique Monfray; and my wife, Nancy, and me, for a car to take us to the awards show. The plan was that we would all meet at Roy and Patty's house in Toluca Lake and from there we would all ride in the limo together. It was a nice way to kick off the evening and it was an opportunity for all of us to be together once more, since the film had been completed nearly a year earlier.

I had put together twelve matted images of the two Fate Heads coming together from the film, along with a copy of the sheet music for *Destino* and brought those to Roy and Patty's home that evening. Roy, Dominique, Baker, and I signed all of them, and we each kept one for ourselves,

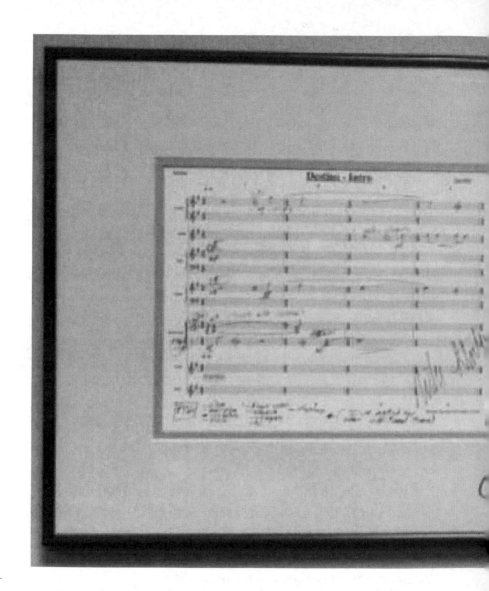

*Roy, Dominique Monfray, Baker Bloodworth, and Dave Bossert
signed this* Destino *memento, and eleven others just like it, in
Roy and Patty's home in Toluca Lake February 29, 2004, just
before being whisked away in a limo to the Seventy-sixth Academy
Awards show.*

and the others were given out as gifts, including one to Ed Nowak.

Roy, Dominique, and their respective guests were in the orchestra-level seats. Nancy and I were in the first balcony looking down on them. We had all agreed, as we parted ways for our seats, to meet up in the main lobby at the end of the show regardless of the outcome.

At that year's show there were five films nominated in the Best Animated Short category: *Destino* (Disney), *Boundin'* (Pixar), *Gone Nutty*, *Nibbles*, and *Harvey Krumpet*. We were disappointed when the winner was announced: *Harvey Krumpet*, a stop-motion film from Australia.

Roy told me later that as the envelope was opened and the name was just being read onstage, he actually grabbed the armrests of his seat as if to get up. When he realized that *Destino* wasn't the winner, he sunk back into his seat and told me he was really disappointed.

When the awards show ended, we made our way to the main lobby. By the time Nancy and I arrived in the lobby, Roy and Patty were mingling. The crowd was starting to thin—some with those holding Academy Governor's Ball tickets were heading to the grand ballroom for the main after-party. All nominees, presenters, and the usual VIPs get tickets to the Governor's Ball. Roy and Dominique, along with their guests, had tickets, but Nancy and I didn't.

Roy asked the question that was on everyone's mind: "What do you want to do?" No one really said anything, so Roy turned to Patty and said, "What do you want to do?" Patty promptly replied that she would like to get out of there and go to In-N-Out for some burgers and fries. That answer provoked an outburst of laughter, and everyone loved the plan.

When we pulled into In-N-Out Burger, we discovered that the drive-through lane would not accommodate our stretch limousine. Our driver didn't realize that, and he spent several minutes trying to back out of the lane. While he was working the car out of the tight spot, some of us got out of the car in the parking lot and went inside to place our order.

Food in hand, we headed for Roy and Patty's home. The burgers and fries were distributed around the dining room. Patty made sure that we all had whatever we needed: ketchup, utensils, water, and glasses. Roy broke out a magnum of red wine that happened to be from John and the Lasseter Family Winery.

So there we all were having just come from the Academy Awards and we were chowing down on burgers and drinking an excellent bottle of red. Our disappointment was soon forgotten as we enjoyed each other's company into the wee hours of the morning.

Roy E. Disney during the nature film years

Roy loved nature!

Chapter 8
True Life Separation

In April 2006 I went to the Van Nuys Airport to meet up with Roy for a flight to Orlando to film the introductions for the True-Life Adventures DVD sets.

I was one of the first to arrive and I waited in the hangar's

True-Life Adventures logo

A young Roy E. Disney in his office at the Burbank Studio lot

lounge area for Roy and the others to arrive. It wasn't too long before Roy arrived, and his oldest son, Roy Pat, was with him. We didn't know that Roy Pat was joining us, but we were happy that he was there. It would give us the opportunity to include him with his dad in one or more of the bonus pieces that we were shooting.

There was an uncomfortable air about Roy and Roy Pat. It was clear something was going on. Roy Pat came over to me and told me that his parents, Roy and Patty, had just separated the night before. Apparently Roy left the house with just the clothes on his back and little money in his pocket.

The split appeared to have been building for a while, but it was still a shock. Patty and Roy had been married for more than fifty years.

Roy had no extra clothes or luggage with him when he arrived. A Shamrock Holdings employee, Kathleen Galli, came to the hangar and gave Roy $300 cash so that he would have some pocket money. Roy Pat had made the last-minute decision to come on the trip so that he could spend some time with his father.

We boarded the plane, the door was closed, we took our seats, and the plane began to taxi to the runway.

Once at our cruising altitude, I was up getting something to drink when Roy came over to me. He asked if there were any way that we could put Roy Pat in some of the pieces that we were planning on shooting in Orlando. I smiled and told him that I was one step ahead of him and that I already had that discussion with David Jessen and Les Perkins and we had already started planning on that. Roy smiled and said thank you; he was very happy that Roy Pat would be included.

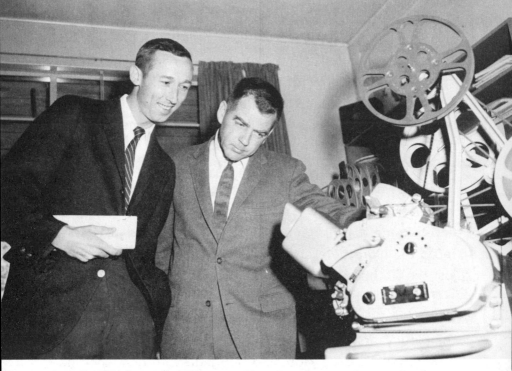

Roy with True-Life Adventures film editor Norman "Stormy" Palmer

Roy and Norman "Stormy" Palmer looking at some film in studio editorial

Roy at Burbank Studio during the making of
The Owl That Didn't Give a Hoot, *circa 1968*

Roy absolutely loved the Animal Kingdom Park and went to it any chance he got. It was only natural that we decided to film the introductions to the True-Life Adventures at that Disney park.

Filming the introductions with Roy at Disney's Animal Kingdom was not a done deal. Because of the tight budget we had, I started a discussion with a parks "synergy" person to see if we could get the parks on board with us shooting the intros at Disney's Animal Kingdom. We were looking for the park to cover our travel, hotel rooms, and meals in exchange for featuring the Animal Kingdom throughout the DVD collection. It would be a terrific promotion for the park and save us a lot on our budget.

Through a bunch of discussions back and forth, it basically came down to the fact that there was no way that the Florida park was going to pay for our airfare to Orlando. It was just too much and it would break their marketing budget for that fiscal year. Travel to Florida was the deal breaker.

I had the unenviable task of telling Roy that we could not do the shoot at Disney's Animal Kingdom because the budget just couldn't support it. I called Roy and told him the bad news that we couldn't afford the airfare for the team; it just wasn't going to work with the budget we had.

He was clearly disappointed but also understood the budget situation. I did my best in suggesting that we could shoot in a bunch of great locations around Southern California and that we could really make it look great. But we both knew that it wouldn't be the same and that it was going to be a terribly missed opportunity for the park.

I don't even think twenty-four hours had passed since that phone call with Roy when he called to say, "Dave, I was thinking . . . what if I flew everyone down to Orlando on my dime? The only thing I would ask is that they [the parks] pick up our hotel rooms and food. What do you think?"

What did I think? Awesome! It was like your buddy calling you up and saying, "Hey, let's go on a road trip, and I'll drive," but instead of an old, beat-up station wagon, it's a Boeing 737 airplane!

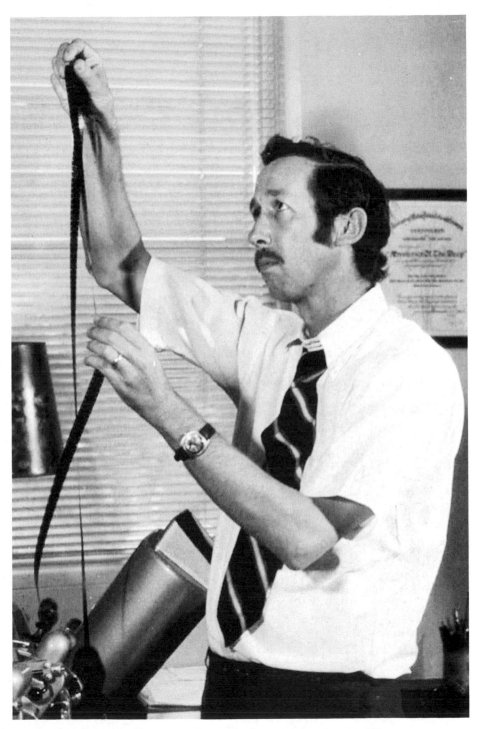

Roy in studio editorial looking at some nature film

Roy at a True-Life Adventures DVD signing event

Disney's Animal Kingdom cheetah exam;
Roy (center) is with Dr. Beth Stevens (who's to his left).

How generous he was to offer to fly us all down to Orlando on his private jet. He certainly didn't have to do that and no one asked him to do it; he just wanted to make the True-Life Adventures DVD the best it could be and he knew that shooting at Disney's Animal Kingdom was the right thing to do: it was quality.

My next step was to get back on the phone with the synergy guy and figure out how we were going to make this work now that the airfare issue was off the table. I explained the fact that Roy would be flying us all down to Orlando and that he was picking up that cost, but that our expectation was that the park would cover our hotel rooms and food while we were there for the shoot.

Several days later he got back to me to say that the park would cover all the hotel rooms, but could only cover Roy's meals. The rest of us travelling would have to take care of ourselves.

About a week later I went over to Roy's office to give him an update on how our plans were progressing. I told him that all the rooms were being covered by the park, but that only his meals would be covered. He furrowed his brow and looked at me and said, "Seriously?" And without missing a beat I asked him if he wouldn't mind picking up dinner every night for all us, to which he burst out laughing and said, "Sure thing." And we both had a really great laugh.

Once we arrived in Orlando and had all checked into our respective hotel rooms, we had decided on a time to meet for dinner.

Since Roy didn't have any clothing with him, David Jessen and I went out to the Downtown Disney shopping district to get a selection of shirts and pants that Roy could wear during the film shoots. I sent Roy an e-mail asking about his shirt and pant sizes, and he promptly sent me back the following note:

Hi Dave:

Pants are 38 waist (with some elastic!!!) . . . 29 inseam if that matters . . . and I usually wear an XL polo shirt . . . hope that helps . . . see you in the morning.

—Roy

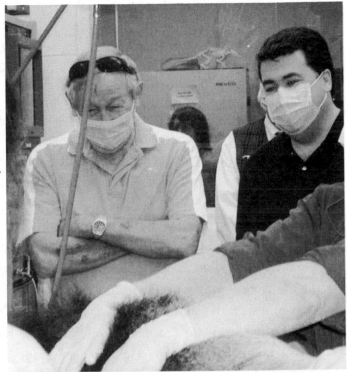

Roy and Dave Bossert (right) observing a tooth extraction on a silverback gorilla (below) at Disney's Animal Kingdom Park Veterinarian clinic

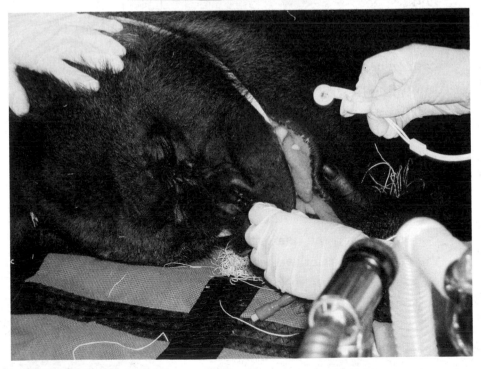

We found a number of tropical, nature-looking shirts and bought enough to cover the various "locations" that we would be shooting at in Disney's Animal Kingdom.

We started our first day of shooting at the Veterinarian center at the Animal Kingdom Park. We were going to be filming an annual exam on a cheetah, with the veterinarian explaining what and why they were doing the examination. Roy and Roy Pat would be asking some questions during this segment.

While the crew was getting set up in the examination room, which had a glass wall so that park guests could view what was going on as part of the overall experience of being at the park, I was with Roy discussing what we wanted to accomplish with this shoot. While we were talking, I noticed that his eyelids were drooping a bit, sort of to half mast, and I asked him if he was okay. He said he was feeling a bit dizzy and needed to sit down, so I pulled a chair up. He asked for a peanut butter sandwich and some milk, and told me that his blood sugar was dropping and that it had been happening on and off for a while. Roy finished his peanut butter sandwich and the milk and was back to his normal self and ready to do the shoot in the examination room.

Jessen and I were concerned enough about this that we asked that they have a paramedic unit nearby at each location of the park that we would be shooting at; we didn't want to take any chances with Roy having a medical emergency. So, the park representative that was assigned to us made sure that just behind the nearest cast member entrance/exit to the backstage area there was a paramedic unit parked. The parks typically have medical personnel strategically placed out of sight of the guest, because when you have tens of

TOP SECRET
YETI EVIDENCE FILE

DOC. NO.: 1464

SCRIPTION: Last known photo of tourist
expedition. Current where abouts
of passenger unknown

DO NOT REMOVE
FROM EVIDENCE FOLDER

EXPEDITION
EVEREST
2006

Riding Everest at Disney's Animal Kingdom:
front row: Roy E. Disney and Roy P. Disney;
middle row: Dave Bossert and Alex McMichael;
back row: Tye Arnold and Les Perkins

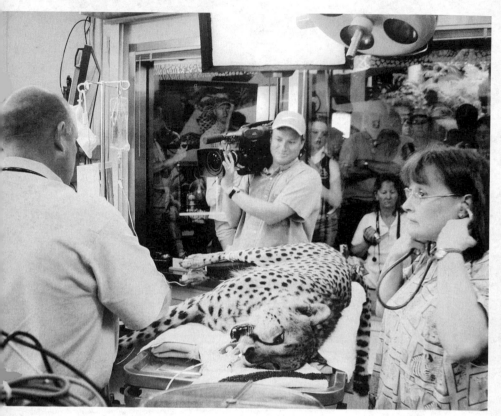

Park guests behind glass had a chance to see the cheetah exam while we were filming.

thousands of people visiting your parks daily, there is always a chance for a medical emergency to happen.

Later that same day, we were shooting at an outdoor location near Expedition Everest. The location allowed for us to shoot in one direction for one look and then just turn our camera setup around and shoot an entirely different setting. It was an optimal location for us to work efficiently without taxing Roy.

After shooting one of the intros, we took a break while

the crew shifted the camera and lighting setup for the next setting. Roy was going to need to change shirts so as to have a new look for this next introduction, and I asked him if he wanted to go backstage to the restroom to change. He said, "No, I'll just change over here," gesturing to what looked like temple ruins.

Roy just walked over behind this stone structure, out of view of the park's guests, and just proceeded to take off his

Roy Pat, center, with his father checking out the cheetah

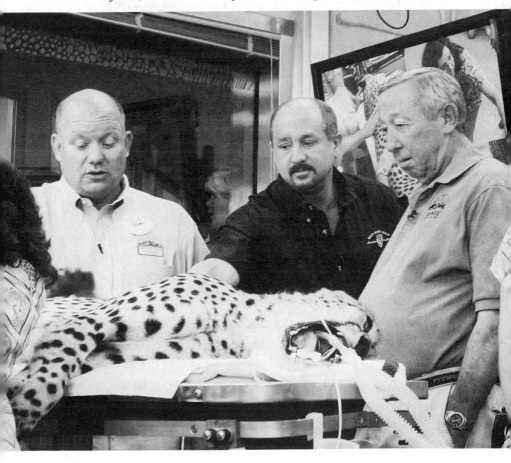

*The True-Life Adventures crew photo with Roy backstage at
the Disney Animal Kingdom Park, 2006*

shirt, which he handed to me, and then put on the new one.
While he was there he decided to unzip his pants and urinate
next to the "ruins," just because it was convenient. It was
completely out of sight of any park guest, and I just turned
away and looked at David Jessen, and we both just gave
each other a smile; it was a sort of a wink and a nod that Roy
was just one of the gang, a regular guy!

At one point during a brief break, Roy asked me if I had
been on Expedition Everest, and I said no because it
had only recently opened. I asked if he had ridden it and

he said, "Oh, yeah, it's awesome! Do you want to go on to it when we're done?"

That said, I was struck by the fact that earlier in the day there was a real concern about Roy's health and that he had gotten dizzy enough that he had almost dropped to the floor, and now he was asking me if I wanted to ride this awesome roller coaster. Of course I would like to go on the ride with him, but I wanted to make sure he was okay to do it.

Roy loved roller coasters. He was seventy-six years old at that point and was like a kid on the ride; at heart he was a bit of a thrill seeker. Roy seemed to be feeling better. We were taking it easy with him and making sure he was hydrated and sitting in the shade between takes.

When we finished filming for the day, Roy popped on some sunglasses and a baseball cap, and a group of us made our way over to Expedition Everest. Normally, we would have waited on the queue, but the park representative assigned to us insisted that we jump the line, and we got right into a ride vehicle. Roy never looked for special treatment, but he didn't argue and was thrilled by the Everest trip.

Roy in Hawaii

Chapter 9
New Beginnings

In early 2008, Roy married his second wife, Leslie DeMeuse, in a private ceremony in Hawaii. They had known each other for a number of years and were producing a new sailing film called *Morning Light* about a group of teens and young adults with varied backgrounds who train together to compete in the Transpac ocean race from Newport, California, to Hawaii.

Roy seemed to be very happy, happier than many of us had seen before, and he looked great. He had stopped chain-smoking nonfiltered cigarettes years earlier and was really taking care of himself thanks to Leslie.

He was in love; he and Leslie were building a new house in Hawaii, and they appeared to be having a ball. Anytime that I visited Roy at his Shamrock office he would invariably show me the progress on the house via a webcam. He was enamored with new technologies.

Leslie and Roy at their wedding in Hawaii
PHOTOS COURTESY OF LESLIE AND ROY DISNEY

Roy and Leslie enjoy a Hawaiian sunset.

Roy and Leslie in Hawaii

Roy at Diamond Head, on Hawaii's Oahu Island;
he and Leslie enjoyed hiking to the top frequently.

Leslie DeMeuse Disney in her own words:

In spite of his last name, wealth, and accomplishments, Roy was the most down to earth and humble "human being" that I have ever known in my entire life.

What made him so lovable and admirable was that he sincerely thought of himself as "just a regular guy," which seemed surprising, but it was probably one of his most endearing qualities, because he made others feel so comfortable being around him. Roy treated everyone with equal kindness, consideration, and respect, no matter who it was or where one came from. It didn't matter. He loved people and would never put himself above someone else because of his name or power.

I often did the on-camera interviews, mostly with very talented competitors, many who were also quite affluent. It was always refreshing to interview someone as authentic and unassuming as Roy. He would never boast about himself on-camera or try to flatter me. I could count on him just to be himself and give me an interview that was interesting without all the fluff.

As a television producer covering yacht racing for thirty plus years, I often wondered if his upbringing had anything to do with his respectable demeanor. After getting to know him over three decades, it became very clear to me he was not raised with a silver spoon, as one might assume he was with a last name like Disney. To the contrary, he was brought up with midwestern values, by parents who were honest and hardworking. Roy would often describe his parents as very affectionate and loving, but tough as nails if he got out of line, especially his mom, who had a no-nonsense attitude.

Roy admitted, as a child he nearly wet his pants a few times trying to fib to his mom, who could read him like a book and would stop him flat in his tracks if he didn't tell the God-honest truth. It soon made sense to me why Roy would often blush if he attempted to sway the truth, even one iota. All I had to do was give him an extra glance and I would get the full and complete story.

He couldn't help but be completely honest, which was one of the many reasons he earned my trust over so many years. He was also open about his shortcomings, which I found commendable.

Roy found great enjoyment for very simple things in life, too. I was quite amused that he loved shopping at Costco with me. Nothing made him happier than to sit down on one of those bright red picnic tables amongst hundreds of other people to have his favorite hotdog and Diet Coke.

To our amazement, no one ever recognized Roy. Of course, who would ever expect someone like Roy E. Disney would be hanging out at a place like

Costco? It soon became one of our favorite places to "hide out in plain sight" because we could sit there for hours and talk without any interruptions. Some of our most delightful times and most meaningful conversations took place at Costco, including a marriage proposal.

It really didn't matter where we were or what we were doing, Roy always made life amusing and fun. He was witty and wise . . . and underneath it all, a big kid at heart. He was the wind in my sails, the spirit in my heart that made my entire life light up

Roy and Leslie in Kona, Hawaii.
PHOTO BY MIKE DANZELSON

with brilliant colors. I will never, ever forget
life with Roy. The spirit of his essences is forever
embedded in my heart and soul.

In late 2008, Roy came by my office for a visit. I asked him why he wasn't coming around the Animation Building much anymore, and he said, in a somewhat melancholy tone, "I don't get invited!" Seriously, his name is on the door and he was not being invited to screenings anymore. He kind of shrugged it off, but I could tell that it bothered him a little.

As we continued to talk, I asked him what he thought about the company and the direction things were going in. He was pleased and seemed content with things; he thought CEO Bob Iger was doing a really great job and that the company was doing very well. He was happy that John Lasseter was back at the company overseeing animation. Roy seemed comfortable with the state of the company. He looked up at me from where he was sitting and said, "Well, I kind of feel like the Lone Ranger riding off into the sunset."

It was a memorable moment in that I think he felt it was time to let go; that there wasn't any more that he could or should do. Roy had fought the good fights and prevailed; he stuck to the values instilled in him by parents and by his own moral compass to look after his family's legacy. He saved the company twice and that was more than most could have mustered in a lifetime.

In early January of 2009, after the holidays, I called Roy to say hi and to see if he wanted to drop by the studio for a visit. Seeing Roy in the Animation Building made everyone light up, and it was always a great treat for everyone.

Roy wasn't in and I left a message with his assistant, Monica Ellsbury, to have him give me a call when he had a chance. I have known Monica for many years, and she seemed to have an edge of concern to her voice when we spoke. I didn't think anything of it at the time other than she was preoccupied with something else.

A few days had passed and I had not heard from Roy, which was unusual as he was great about responding to e-mails and calls. So I called him again at his Shamrock Holdings office and spoke to Monica. She had that air of concern again as we spoke but did not let on that anything was amiss. I left another message for him to give me a call when he had a chance.

Another day or so went by and Roy called me at my office and we exchanged a few pleasantries. Roy told me that he was sorry for not getting back to me sooner and that he was at the doctor a number of times. Then he dropped a bombshell: he had been diagnosed with stomach cancer. My heart dropped; I had so much empathy for him at that moment and wanted to be there for him in any way possible.

Roy wanted to keep this information private, and outside of the immediate family and close friends, nobody knew about it at that point. He wanted to keep it that way as much as possible because he was, in many respects, a very private person.

Roy sounded very upbeat and optimistic about his prognosis; he said he was "going to beat it" and that he had some great doctors. He was relaxed and once again seemed up for the fight.

During the next couple of months, Roy was seeing various doctors and had to do some chemotherapy to get the cancer under control before he could have surgery. Those first few months he did really well, and bounced back from any side effects.

He told me in a phone conversation that he would be having his entire stomach removed— which was shocking to me. He said that it was actually no big deal and that there are people who have done this type of surgery electively for weight loss.

In May, he would drop by the Disney Studio lot for an interview and a few other meetings. It would turn out to be his final visit to the property that he'd virtually grown up at and where he'd spent more than fifty years of his professional working life.

Don Hahn in his own words:

It was May 13, 2009, and I was in the middle of production on Waking Sleeping Beauty, *a documentary about the rebirth of Disney Animation, which in essence was Roy's story. I needed to interview him for the film. I'd decided that the film would be made entirely from archival footage with contemporary voice-over, my way of taking the audience back and placing them in the rooms that we were all so lucky to have been in. I'd had extraordinary cooperation from Jeffrey Katzenberg, and hesitant but willing cooperation from Michael Eisner to do interviews; now it was Roy's turn. He had been sick for quite some time, but had a strong constitution and an unstoppable attitude about beating cancer.*

Roy showed up on time as always. He'd driven to the studio himself and came up to my office in the old Animation Building to talk. I hadn't seen him in awhile and when he sat down and started small talk, it washed over me that this was the guy who shepherded Disney Animation through some rough seas and always stood up for us and our work. For years his office was just a few yards away, and it was so nostalgic to hear him talk about being here again.

Before we recorded, Roy wanted to get a haircut on the roof. The Roof was a men's club where once you could get a grilled sandwich, play cards, work out with weights, and have your hair cut. The club had turned coed in the seventies and now was used as a storeroom except for the barbershop, which was soon to close. Roy took a seat in the reclining barber chair like he had so many times before. The conversation turned to the new health club that was opening on the lot and a hair salon that would soon replace this 1930s barber chair. Roy got a clip and exchanged stories about the business and the old days at the studio. He was never a guy to dwell in the past. He just enjoyed talking and visiting with the people on the lot who had become his family over so many years.

A short walk away was "B Stage," where nearly all of the dialogue for the last seventy years of films had been recorded. I remember Roy recording John

Huston on this stage decades ago as the narrator for
The Black Cauldron. *Since then the cast of*
The Lion King, Beauty and the Beast, Aladdin, *and*
The Little Mermaid *had all stood and recorded*
here in this room. Roy took a seat at a table with a
microphone overhead. Our sound mixer, Doc, came in
and adjusted the microphone and said hi. I sat across
from Roy to ask questions and elicit memories from
his years at the studio. We rolled tape. I started at
the beginning, asking about his earliest memories of
his dad and Walt. He related the night when he was a
little boy and was sick in bed. Walt came up and
told him the entire story of Pinocchio *while acting*
out all the parts. When he saw the film he was so
disappointed because it didn't live up to the
story that Walt told that night at his bedside.

We talked about the nature films and his early
forays into producing. When the conversation turned
to the eighties and nineties, Roy had a particular
twinkle in his eye. Of all his accomplishments, he
knew that he had saved the company from corporate
raiders and then championed an animation
renaissance that built the modern animation
industry. His memories of late-night meetings with
his attorney Stanley Gold and Disney president Frank
Wells could be a subject for an epic novel or comic
opera, depending upon the story. The rise-from-the-
ashes story of Disney Animation was something he
took great pride in. He talked at length about the

price of fame and how money and success started
to affect people. He talked about the artists who
deserved all the credit.

The issue of credit was a very personal one
for Roy and a major stumbling block in his
relationship with studio head Jeffrey Katzenberg. As
Roy talked about credit, it became clear that credit
was an issue in his house growing up. Roy O.
Disney, his dad, had to listen to a constant litany
of complaints about Walt getting all the credit,
and Roy didn't want that to happen again in
the modern age. "Animation is a team sport
and the idea of anyone claiming credit for the
accomplishment is preposterous," he said.

My next question was really a comment.
Animation head Peter Schneider had always said,
"Never underestimate Roy." I told Roy that in my
interview with Jeffrey, he had regretted that he
didn't manage his relationship with Roy better. Roy
smiled. He could have said something very smarmy,
but didn't. Twenty years had passed since Jeffrey left
the company, and, for whatever had happened then,
it wasn't worth it to Roy to open old wounds.

The last thing I asked Roy was why? Why the
takeover of the studio, the fights with shareholders,
the resignations? His answer was pretty simple: when
your name is Disney, you can't stand by and not
participate. "All these things we did," he said, "were
always possible through even the worst of times with

the right people and the right motivations. You just had to keep believing that it's in here [pointing to his heart] . . . you can do it . . . you know it's inside of you. . . ."

The session broke up and Howard Green, our friend and longtime studio publicist, came in with a stack of drawings from the animators on The Princess and the Frog, *each wishing Roy well. Outside the soundstage we jumped into a golf cart and rode across Riverside Drive to the Animation Building to take a look at a 3-D test clip from* Fantasia/2000. *As 3-D was becoming the rage, we had transformed the "Firebird Suite" sequence of* Fantasia *into 3-D for Roy to see the possibilities.*

He was thrilled with the results and left the building smiling and shaking hands with well-wishers. It was a wonderful sun-soaked day. It turned out to be Roy's last visit to the studio, to the Animation Building, to the barber, and to the recording stage. It was his last time on the studio lot that he loved so much and the last day that someone with the last name "Disney" worked there.

Roy had the surgery as scheduled and everything went well according to the doctors. He came through the surgery with flying colors and had this serious part behind him. It was now going to be several more rounds of chemo and radiation that he needed to make sure that they got all the cancer.

Just a few weeks after Roy had his surgery, he responded to one of my e-mails with a note to give me an update on how he was doing. You can tell from the e-mail that he was in great spirits and was on the road to recovery. He was even keeping up with the latest Pixar release *Up*, which was playing in theaters.

6/11/2009—E-mail from Roy

Hi Dave:

Sorry to be so hard to get . . . we've just been really busy, between so many doctors, coming home, getting acclimated to that, etc. . . . and I'm still a bit low on energy . . . but we're doing really well, thank Heaven . . . the doctors are all very pleased with how it all came out (literally, they got ALL the cancer!!), and with the pace of my recovery. We're even planning to go to Hawaii Sunday, for a few days.

We'd love a visit but we'll be away all next week . . . maybe the week after that, though? Any time we're here and it's convenient for you would be great.

How's everything with you and the old stomping grounds? *Up* is sure doing wonderful business. . . .

Talk soon,

—Roy

Throughout the entire ordeal that Roy was going through, Leslie was there by his side. Most importantly, she was keeping a watchful eye on Roy and making sure that he was being well taken care of in all respects. She was so great in keeping all his friends and colleagues up to date on his progress and recovery. Good or bad, she sent out regular update notes via e-mail. Leslie was nothing short of wonderful for Roy.

7/2/2009—Update on Roy from Leslie

Just a quick update. It has been sort of scary this week from the chemo treatment Roy received 11 days ago. It put him in the hospital last Saturday evening. This particular chemo really knocked him down. He hadn't been able to eat anything since 11 days ago . . . not even fluids and he was completely dependent on the feeding tube and IV hydration. His white blood cell count went down to zero. It has been a really frightening week.

But, yesterday, his white blood cell count showed signs of creeping back up! Still, he has very little immunity to infection right now, so he can't have visitors (outside of family) for a few more days. But, yesterday he was eating real food and doing very well! His color has improved a lot! His strength is leaps and bounds better. We got him out of bed and walked him around the entire floor. He was smiling and winking at all the good looking nurses! In spite of the fact it drives me nuts, this is a really GOOD sign. It means his spirits are back! He has been talking on the phone and answering e-mails and he is back to doing his crossword puzzles and thinking about Transpac!

This is ALL REALLY GOOD NEWS!!

—Leslie

Roy, with Leslie, recovering from chemo
at their nearly finished home in Hawaii

The chemo that Roy was getting was really doing a number on him. His son Roy Patrick told me at one point that he thought his father wasn't going to make it through it, because he had had such a bad reaction to the chemo. By the end of July, Roy was quickly bouncing back from the bad reaction that he had in the early part of the month. We traded some e-mails, and he was looking forward to the Transpac race but was not going to be able to participate this year because of his health situation. But he was looking forward to it, nonetheless, so that he could cheer on his son who would be sailing Roy's beloved *Pyewacket*.

7/30/2009—E-mail back from Roy

Hi Dave:

  We're doing fine now, actually quite fine, but you heard right about the last chemo dose a month ago . . . it was like being run over by a Mack truck!

  Next up is radiation, six weeks of it . . . which they tell me won't be such a catastrophe (and I am already mostly bald!).

  We got to Hawaii for the end of the race . . . Roy Pat sailed the boat over and got third in class and fifth in fleet . . . really did well. We put off the house blessing because it's just not close enough to finished yet. Maybe in September . . .

  We're in and out a lot—doctor stuff and back to Hawaii next week—until the last couple of weeks in August . . . so better then . . . but would love to see you and do some catching up.

  Meantime, all our best,

—Roy and Leslie

During this time I was mostly trading e-mails with Roy and occasionally talking with him on the phone. He was spending most of his time at his home in Newport Beach, California, and was getting his treatments at the Hoag Hospital there.

  I had been keeping him abreast of what was going on around the studio and the progress we were making on the restoration and preservation of *Fantasia*. It was one of Roy's favorite films, and we were doing an extensive, back to the original nitrate negative restoration of the film. It was bringing the film back to a spectacular state, and I wanted to try and get Roy up to see some of the dailies. He was excited about it and wanted to see some of it but didn't know when he could come up between the doctors, the chemo, radiation, and jaunts to Hawaii.

In late October, just before Halloween, Roy sent an e-mail note addressed to my wife, Nancy, and me, thanking us for the well-wishes and giving us an optimistic update.

10/29/2009—E-mail from Roy

Hi Dave and Nancy:

Thanks for the note and all your good wishes! I am indeed on the SLOW road back from all the chemo and radiation, not to mention incidental surgery, with high hopes and still a loooong way to go to get back to "normal." But we'll make it.

I for one can't wait to see the *Fantasia* restoration . . . I can imagine there are obstacles galore! And nice to see *Destino* still attracting attention. . . .

I have no idea right now when we'll make it up to Burbank next, but almost certainly not for the *Frog* wrap party . . . I hope it's as good as I've been hearing!!?!

Hawaii is—of course—super; we may never come back!

Hope we see you soon . . . and Aloha!

—Roy and Leslie

We traded several more e-mails into late November, and, by then, Roy and Leslie had returned from Hawaii just after Thanksgiving. During a checkup with the doctors they discovered that Roy's cancer had returned and with a vengeance. It was swift and aggressive.

Roy was admitted to Hoag Hospital in Newport Beach, where he would spend the last days of this life, surrounded by his immediate family. He was a fighter until the end, and was always optimistic that things would be better and that he would beat this terrible disease.

As I mentioned at the outset of this book, Roy succumbed to the cancer on the morning of Wednesday, December 16, 2009. I was at the rerecording session of several Oliver Wallace scores for some 1930s Disney shorts at Capitol Records, and I announced the sad news to our conductor and band members.

Shortly thereafter, Bob Iger sent out an e-mail message to all of the company cast members breaking the news of Roy's passing.

12/16/2009—Note from Bob Iger, CEO of The Walt Disney Company

Dear Cast Members,

It is with great sadness that I inform you of the passing of our friend and colleague Roy E. Disney. After a courageous year-long fight with stomach cancer, he passed away peacefully this morning at

Roy and his daughter Susan in Hawaii during Thanksgiving 2009; this was taken just two weeks before he passed away. Susan recalls having "a really nice time with him and that he was in heaven at his house there."

Hoag Hospital in Newport Beach, surrounded by his loving family.

Roy played an important role in our lives here at Disney, and in the success of our Company over many years. Along the way, he touched many of us in a personal way. During his 56-year association with the Company, his true passion and focus was preserving and building upon the amazing legacy of Disney animation that was started by his father and uncle. His commitment to the art of animation was unparalleled and will always remain his personal legacy and one of the greatest contributions to Disney's past, present, and future.

Roy not only helped to keep the legacy alive, but he also embraced new technologies, and gave the filmmakers the tools they needed to tell their stories in new and exciting ways. He encouraged talent, and loved working with the creative community. And they loved working with him.

Roy was a Disney Legend in every sense of the word, and his contributions to this great company have been profound and will always be remembered. For the next week we will be flying the Disney flag at half mast here at the studio and at our parks, and I know you join me in sending thoughts and prayers to Roy's wife, Leslie, his four children, and his sixteen grandchildren. For those who wish to pay their respects, the family has requested that donations be made in Roy's name to the California International Sailing Association (CISA) to benefit youth sailing.

—Bob

Roy was cremated and some of his ashes were spread in the Pacific Ocean off the coast of Newport Beach at the starting area of the Transpac sailing race he so loved; another portion of his ashes were spread at the finish line off the coast of Honolulu, Hawaii. The remainder were sprinkled at the top of Diamondhead on the Hawaiian island of Oahu, where Roy and Leslie liked to hike.

When the family spread some of Roy's ashes off the coast of Newport Beach, his oldest son took a photo of the flowers they dropped into the water. As the flowers floated away they formed a smiley face, which was so apropos in remembering Roy Edward Disney, who often had a smile for those who were lucky enough to know him.

It was the end of an era in which The Walt Disney Company had a Disney family member closely involved. From the time that Walt and his brother Roy Oliver started the Disney

Upside-down smiley face of flowers at the memorial at sea off Newport Beach. **PHOTO BY ROY P. DISNEY**

Brothers Studio in 1923 until Roy Edward's passing in 2009, there had been a Disney closely involved with the company, with the exception of those few periods in which Roy E. had resigned from the Board of Directors. Even then, he did so in order to better the future prospects of the company.

After Roy passed away, a group of us, his studio friends, put material together for a memorial service, which was really a life celebration. The program was being spear-headed by Don Hahn and was held at the Disney-owned El Capitan Theatre on Hollywood Boulevard in Hollywood.

It would be a great send-off for Roy, and everyone attending was encouraged to wear Hawaiian shirts.

Roy had actually given me a Hawaiian shirt many years ago. It had some vintage Mickey images on it and had some-what of a 1940s look to it, and he thought that I would like it. I still have it and very rarely wear it because I want it to last a lifetime. It hangs in my closet, and I see it nearly every day; it reminds me of many good memories with Roy.

Before the life celebration began, Roy's children hosted a breakfast. It was for close friends and colleagues, and there was a festive atmosphere; in a sense it was the beginning of celebrating Roy's life before we headed over to the El Capitan Theatre across the street, for the more formal stage presentations and speeches.

There were a number of memorable moments during the theater presentation, from the stories told by Roy's sailing buddies and studio colleagues to Dick Van Dyke and author John Culhane remembering Roy.

Bob Iger's comments were heartfelt and succinct. At the end he announced that the Walt Disney Animation Studios building would be named after Roy. It was very apropos

The Roy E. Disney Animation Building in Burbank, California

since Roy was largely responsible for igniting what now is widely considered the renaissance of Disney animation: the Second Golden Age.

When Alton Fitzgerald White, a singer, and a choir came out onstage and started performing "He Lives in You," from the Broadway production of *The Lion King*, I don't think

The author Dave with wife Nancy and Roy at CalArts

there was a dry eye in the house. I know that my wife, Nancy, and I got choked up at the spine-tingling performance. It was a wonderful way to conclude Roy's life celebration.

Roy Edward Disney does live in all the people he touched.

He was a man of integrity, sincerity, compassion, and intelligence, an individual who valued quality and acknowledged the team effort. Roy was a rare gift to us all, and I am so very proud to say I was his friend.

Memorial card from the Roy E. Disney life celebration